PENGUIN BOOKS

A Good Childhood

Richard Layard is Emeritus Professor of Economics at the London School of Economics, and author of the bestselling *Happiness* (Penguin, 2005). He was founder-director of the Centre for Economic Performance at the London School of Economics and now heads its programme on Well-being. He is also a member of the House of Lords.

Judy Dunn is Professor of Developmental Psychology at the Institute of Psychiatry, King's College, London. Her research interests are in children's social, emotional and communicative development, studied in their families and with their friends. She is Chair of The Good Childhood Inquiry.

A Good Childhood

Searching for Values in a Competitive Age

RICHARD LAYARD,
JUDY DUNN
and the panel of
The Good Childhood Inquiry

PENGUIN BOOKS

PENGUIN BOOKS

Published by the Penguin Group
Penguin Books Ltd, 80 Strand, London WC2R ORL, England
Penguin Group (USA) Inc., 375 Hudson Street, New York, New York 10014, USA
Penguin Group (Canada), 90 Eglinton Avenue East, Suite 700, Toronto, Ontario, Canada M4P 2Y3
(a division of Pearson Penguin Canada Inc.)
Penguin Ireland, 25 St Stephen's Green, Dublin 2, Ireland
(a division of Penguin Books Ltd)
Penguin Group (Australia), 250 Camberwell Road, Camberwell, Victoria 3124, Australia
(a division of Pearson Australia Group Pty Ltd)
Penguin Books India Pvt Ltd, 11 Community Centre, Panchsheel Park, New Delhi – 110 017, India
Penguin Group (NZ), 67 Apollo Drive, Rosedale, North Shore 0632, New Zealand
(a division of Pearson New Zealand Ltd)
Penguin Books (South Africa) (Pty) Ltd, 24 Sturdee Avenue,
Rosebank, Johannesburg 2196, South Africa

Penguin Books Ltd, Registered Offices: 80 Strand, London WC2R ORL, England

www.penguin.com

First published 2009
6

Set in 12.75/14.75 pt PostScript Monotype Garamond
Typeset by Rowland Phototypesetting Ltd, Bury St Edmunds, Suffolk
Printed in England by Clays Ltd, St Ives plc

A CIP catalogue record for this book is available from the British Library

ISBN: 978-0-141-03943-5

www.greenpenguin.co.uk

Penguin Books is committed to a sustainable future
for our business, our readers and our planet.
The book in your hands is made from paper
certified by the Forest Stewardship Council.

Contents

Preface

This book is about children's experiences of childhood. It is about all children, not a selected group, and it is written for all of us, whatever our calling. It was initiated on the premise that childhood is changing rapidly, and we have a duty to try to understand this change and engage with it in a positive manner. But I want to begin with a story.

Adam is 20 years old now. He was one of the young people who attended a Good Childhood Inquiry panel meeting and spoke with the panel members. The Children's Society first started working with him when he was 14. He told the panel his story. For many working in the childcare system, his story is all too common. Never really experiencing the family love and support that are so important for a good childhood, Adam was taken into care at a young age. He was moved from residential home to residential home and, when that didn't work, into foster care. Actually, nothing worked for Adam and he fought against every attempt to reach out to him. Eventually, he got involved in crime and at age 14 began the first of three sentences in prison.

After hearing his story, one of the panel members asked him whether there was anyone in his life for whom he had praise. It took Adam a few seconds to respond. Then he said that the only person he could think of was his Independent Visitor. This is the person we provided as a contact point for Adam while he was in prison – someone to talk to, to help him think through *his situation and navigate choices as well as plan for his release and next steps. Adam went on to explain that when he was first assigned his Independent Visitor, a support service that he neither requested nor wanted, he treated him just as he had treated everyone else in the many residential homes or foster families in which he had lived. He rebelled against him and used every trick in his book to make the visitor leave and not come back. But it didn't work. For the first time in Adam's life, he had met someone who would not give up on him, who, regardless of the treatment that Adam subjected him to, would come back, week after week after week.*

Adam explained that he eventually decided that if there was nothing he could do to cause his visitor to leave, then he might as well try and make the relationship work. This was the beginning of Adam's first constructive and positive relationship with an adult. Now, six years on, they are still in contact and this relationship provides Adam with a critically important source of stability, from which other positive relationships can grow. Adam is out of prison and determined to make something of his life.

Adam's story is an example of the power of commitment in a relationship with a child. Once it was clear to Adam that at least this one adult would never give up on him or abandon him, he was able to look afresh at himself and start the long journey towards what he himself would consider a productive life.

In Britain today there are far too many stories like Adam's. Child poverty is at unacceptable levels for such an economically advanced nation, too many children are in care, doing poorly at school, in trouble with the law and in prison. It is only in relatively recent times that we have begun to understand the extent of mental health problems across the nation, especially with our youth. This is reason enough for us having The Good Childhood Inquiry – our concern for these groups of children, many of whom suffer multiple disadvantages. But this book is about all children, and it is written to help us understand the state of childhood for all, with a very clear message that, as a nation, we must do more for our children – all of us working together.

The Good Childhood Inquiry is an enormously valuable contribution to our understanding of childhood as it brings together in one place an impressive amount of information, knowledge and views in a way that is easily understood and which directs us to action.

But why is it felt to be so important now? The answer lies not in a presumption that ours is the first generation to show concern for children. Every generation wants to do its best for children. But there is something very special, and very different, about the way in which children experience childhood as we begin the twenty-first century. Every decade brings new developments and changes to society, but the pace of change today is unprecedented. This affects us all, and in the midst of such dramatic change it is our duty to stop and reflect on its impact on children and young people and re-evaluate the place of childhood in modern society.

Some of the most visible examples of change are in information technology and demographics. Advances in technology have provided children (and of course adults) with access to information that would have been unimaginable just a generation ago. Increasing diversity – certainly within Britain, but also in other countries – means that children interact with different cultures, languages, faiths and traditions on a regular basis. One in four children born today in Britain is to a mother who was herself not born here. Some schools and local doctors' surgeries support pupils or patients with a range of over forty or more languages. And, for the first time in history, the number of over-65-year-olds exceeds the number of under-16-year-olds.

These and other changes, and the pace at which they are occurring, need not be viewed with suspicion or as threats. Indeed, change can be celebrated and embraced. But as a society we tend to be wary of change. We feel uncertain about where these changes are leading us and what we will look like as a society in the future. This is precisely why The Good Childhood Inquiry is so important, and so important now. It is because we value children that we need to take this opportunity to listen to the key messages from this book. To listen and discuss – as widely as possible and with as many people as possible. In the book children are referred to as a 'sacred trust'. Indeed they are. We owe it to them, to ourselves and to society to re-address their place and the status of childhood. To put children truly at the centre of our world, now and for ever.

This inquiry is also important now because of the window of opportunity that we have to influence real and positive change for children. As a testament of its significance, more than 35,000 people contributed to the inquiry through the call for evidence, surveys, focus groups, 'my life' postcards and the BBC Newsround television programme. This reflects how strongly the subject of childhood resonates with people at this time. The government has been investing heavily in children's services, through the 'Every Child Matters' programme, since 2002 and has made an inspirational commitment to ending child poverty in Britain by 2020. Therefore, the time is right to draw on the momentum generated by these initiatives and to take the debate further, by using The Good Childhood Inquiry *as a platform for debate and discussion with the public. For if we are to be successful in creating real change for children and a better understanding of modern childhood, then the responsibility rests with all of us, not a select few.*

This book represents The Good Childhood Inquiry panel's discussions over eighteen months during 2007 and 2008. The panel members have agreed that this book reflects fairly the work of the panel, and support the vision and recommendations made herein. The inquiry was designed to achieve consensus, but with the diversity of the panel we did not set out to produce a book where every panel member agreed with every word written. We sought the healthy and necessary tension and difference of view that such an important exercise warrants. Equally, the report does not, in any way, represent the policies or philosophies of the organizations from which the panel members come. Each panel member joined the inquiry in his or her own right and not as a representative of any organization or constituency.

This was an independent inquiry and one that we believe will provide a significant contribution to the thinking and discussion about childhood and its status in society for many years to come.

This book builds on the evidence gathered during its eighteen months of work, but rightly goes further, drawing on the panel's expertise and experience to evaluate and interpret the evidence. The views and recommendations contained in this document are designed to help us all make childhood better.

I would like to take this opportunity to thank sincerely each and every panel member for their time, energy, thought-provoking debate and unquestionable devotion to children and young people. They are:

Professor Judy Dunn (Chair)
Professor Sir Albert Aynsley-Green
Dr Muhammad Abdul Bari
Jim Davis
Professor Philip Graham
Professor Kathleen Kiernan
Professor Lord Richard Layard
Professor Barbara Maughan
Professor Stephen Scott
The Rt Revd Bishop Tim Stevens
Professor Kathy Sylva

The panel explored seven key themes of childhood: family, friends, lifestyle, values, schooling, mental health and inequality. Seven of the panel members took on the role of 'theme leader', which required substantial extra effort in producing research papers for each theme. They are Kathleen Kiernan (family), Judy Dunn (friends), Philip Graham (lifestyle), Tim Stevens (values), Kathy Sylva (schooling) and Barbara Maughan and Stephen Scott (mental health). We are extremely grateful for their dedication to this inquiry. The quality of their research papers helped the panel focus on the key issues to be debated and provided an enormously useful resource for further discussion. All research papers and summaries of the contributions submitted through our call for evidence can be found on our website at www.childrenssociety.org.uk. I strongly urge readers to access this incredibly rich resource.

A very special note of appreciation goes to two panel members: The Chair of The Good Childhood Inquiry, Judy Dunn, and the principal author of the report, Richard Layard. Without their leadership and quiet but strong resolve, the book would not have been produced to the standard that it has. They guided us through the complex evidence, debate and real stories that contribute to what we understand childhood to be and the absolute critical importance that it should have in our world.

Bob Reitemeier
Chief Executive, The Children's Society
November 2008

What are the best things about your life? love.

What are the worst things about your life? arguments.

1. Is There a Problem?

Well I think stop children having a good life is people who
are selfish and only care about themselves.
(11-year-old girl)

In many ways our children have never lived so well.
Materially, they have more possessions, better homes,
more holidays away. They enjoy a whole new world of
technology which brings them music, information, entertainment, and an unprecedented ability to communicate
with their friends. Over 90 per cent of children over 11
have a mobile phone.[1]

Our children are also more educated and less often
sick than ever before. They are more open and honest
about themselves and more tolerant of human diversity
in all its forms.[2] And they are more concerned about the
environment. We are proud of our children and their
accomplishments, and rightly so.

And yet there is also widespread unease about our
children's experience – about the commercial pressures
they face, the violence they are exposed to, the stresses
at school, and the increased emotional distress. Some of
this unease is exaggerated and reflects unwarranted angst
about the greater freedom that children now enjoy. But

some of it reflects a genuine fear on behalf of our children – that somehow their lives are becoming more difficult, and more difficult than they ought to be.

Trends

The survey evidence supports these fears. More young people are anxious and troubled. As the top figure shows, the proportion of 15 to 16-year-olds experiencing significant emotional difficulties rose a lot between 1974 and 1999, since when it has remained roughly stable.[3] In addition, more young people have behavioural problems. As the bottom figure shows, difficult behaviour increased between 1974 and 1999, but has changed little since then.

The figures opposite relate to Britain as a whole. But a separate study of emotional difficulties among 15-year-olds in Scotland showed very similar results.[4] These changes affected teenagers from all social classes, and the worries most often listed were over family relationships, weight and school-work.

These problems are connected with the changing world in which children are growing up. More families now break up and more mothers go out to work. New media, including the Internet, expose children to commercial and lifestyle influences unknown before. The pressure of school exams is greater than ever. And relative poverty affects more children than in most of the last fifty years. These are the influences whose effects we shall be examining in this book.

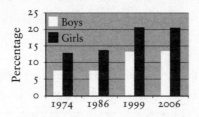

Percentage of 15/16-year-olds suffering from emotional difficulties[3]

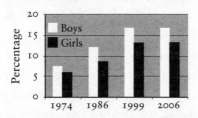

Percentage of 15/16-year-olds suffering from behavioural difficulties[3]

International Differences

But are all countries equally affected? In early 2007 the newspapers were full of the results of a remarkable report commissioned by UNICEF, the children's arm of the United Nations, showing how children are faring in all twenty-one of the world's richest countries.[5] It showed that children in Britain and the US do indeed face a much more difficult world than those in continental Europe. The report began with an overall ranking of the twenty-one countries in which Britain came bottom of the class and the United States next. We can see how this came about by looking in the table opposite at some of the individual items in the index, suitably updated.[6] This allows us to compare Britain and the US with the continental countries of Western Europe. Britain and the US have more broken families than other countries, and our families are less cohesive in the way they live and eat together. British children are rougher with each other, and live more riskily in terms of alcohol, drugs and teenage pregnancy. And they are less inclined to stay in education.

This comes against the background of much greater income inequality: many more children live in relative poverty in Britain and the US. We might worry less about this inequality if Britain and the US were lands of opportunity where someone who was born poor might rise easily. However we are not only more unequal than other advanced countries; we are also less socially mobile than many other countries.[7]

So how far is inequality the cause of our children's problems? Partly, but only partly. Family break-up affects children in all classes, as do the commercial and peer pressures that encourage risky lifestyles. And exam pressures bear if anything more heavily on middle-class than working-class children. But we believe there is one common theme that links all these problems: excessive individualism. This was also identified as the leading social evil in the Joseph Rowntree Foundation's consultation on 'social evils'.[8]

Measures of child welfare[6]

	Britain	USA	Other Western European countries
Families			
% in step-families (aged 11–15)	12	14	8
% in single-parent families (aged 11–15)	16	24	14
% eating main meal with parents less than 'several times a week' (aged 15)	33	34	17
Friends			
% involved in a physical fight in last year (aged 11–15)	41	36	37
Lifestyle			
% overweight (aged 11–15)	13	29	13
% who have been drunk at least twice (aged 13–15)	33	12	18
% who used cannabis in last 12 months (aged 15)	19	22	13
% of women (aged 15–19) giving birth per year	2.5	5	1
% of 15-year-olds who have had sex	29		27
Schooling			
% not in education (aged 15–19)	22	21	15
% not in education or work (aged 15–19)	9	6	6
Inequality			
% with income less than 60% of the median (aged 0–17)	22	29	16

Excessive Individualism

By excessive individualism we mean the belief that the prime duty of the individual is to make the most of her own life, rather than to contribute to the good of others. Of course, some degree of individualism is necessary for survival, and individual choice and self-determination are vital ingredients of a good life. But individuals will never lead satisfying lives except in a society where people care for each other and promote each other's good as well as their own. The pursuit of personal success *relative* to others cannot create a happy society, since one person's success necessarily involves another's failure.[9]

Individual freedom and self-determination bring many blessings, but they can only exist if balanced by a proper sense of care and responsibility for others. That is the basic idea of individual rights matched by corresponding responsibilities for others, on which modern society depends. But in Britain and the US the balance has tilted too far towards the individual pursuit of private interest and success.[10] So it is excessive individualism, we believe, that is causing a whole range of problems for our children: high family break-up, teenage unkindness, unprincipled advertising, too much competition in education and, of course, our acceptance of income inequality. One major theme of this report is the need for a more caring ethic and for less aggression – for, to put it bluntly, a society more based upon the law of love.

An inscription on a tablet dated around 2800 BC reads:

'Children no longer obey their parents. Every man wants to write a book, and the end of the world is evidently approaching.'[11] People have always been prone to imagine a golden age which never existed. But the sad fact is that individualism has increased in our society.

The clearest evidence of this is that people trust each other less than they used to. At various times people have been asked: 'Would you say that most people can be trusted – or would you say that you can't be too careful in dealing with people?' In 1959, 56 per cent of Britons said yes, most people could be trusted. By 1999 that figure had roughly halved, as the table shows.

Percentage saying that most people can be trusted (Britain)[12]	
1959	56
1981	43
1990	44
1999	29

The Children's Society's survey supports this evidence. A representative sample of adults was asked whether today's children had a stronger sense of moral values than in the past or was it not as strong.[13] Only 7 per cent said stronger and 66 per cent said not as strong. Similarly, when asked whether today's children had a stronger sense of community than in the past, only 5 per cent said stronger and 69 per cent said not as strong.

The same trends can be seen in the United States, where the percentage saying that most people can be trusted has been almost the same in different years as that we have shown for Britain – with the same fall in trust.[14] In addition, US adults have been asked whether they think people lead 'as good lives – moral and honest – as they used to'. In 1952 50 per cent thought that people were as moral as they used to be. By 1998 this figure had fallen to 27 per cent.

There was of course no golden age, but something has changed for the worse. And the change began among adults. When some newspapers demonize children and young people, as they often do, they should think more deeply about the causes of this malaise. And they should also do more to reflect the wonderful, positive aspects of their lives.

For this book is not a dirge. Quite the opposite. Children aged 11–16 have been asked the following question, and their replies are displayed below the possible answers:[15]

Which best describes how you feel about your life as a whole?[15]

Completely happy			Neither happy nor unhappy			Completely unhappy
36%	34%	17%	9%	2%	1%	1%

So, according to this survey, a lot of children are happy. But 13 per cent are less than happy, which means one and a half million children, and 17 per cent are only just happy. There are causes to celebrate *and* causes to worry.

8

Our Approach

So our report starts from the basic power for good inherent in children,[16] and their extraordinary potential. It asks what they need to flourish, and what are the obstacles to their flourishing. And chapter by chapter it makes striking and imaginative recommendations about how they could lead better and more fulfilled lives.

Flourishing means above all social engagement and the enjoyment of life – fulfilling our capacity to live in harmony with others and with ourselves. Children flourish when they have a sense of meaning in their lives, which comes both from social engagement and from enthusiastic development of their own interests and talents. Children need both outer and inner harmony. These complement each other: outer harmony comes from a spirit of giving, and inner self-worth makes getting less of an imperative.

Children who grow up like this are likely to lead happy lives. They will not be happy all the time. But they will learn to treat a setback as a challenge, and eventually to rise above it. And they will contribute to the happiness of others.

What Children Need

So what in concrete terms do our children need in order to flourish? If we look at their lives as they develop, seven elements stand out:

- They need **loving families**, where they observe and experience love, and thus learn how to love others. They also need boundaries to be set by parents who are firm but not dictatorial.
- They need **friends**, as they begin to explore outside the family. From developing their friendships, they learn many of the basic lessons of living.
- They need a positive **lifestyle**, in which they develop interests which satisfy them and avoid the enticements of excessive commercialism and unhealthy living.
- Such a lifestyle can only be built on solid **values**, which give meaning to life and are acquired from parents, schools, media, political and faith organizations.
- Children need **good schools**, where they can acquire both values and competence.
- They need good **mental health**, and children with difficulties need help.
- And they need **enough money** to live among their peers without shame.

Easy to say, but what a challenge to achieve. To give children what they need is in fact the greatest challenge facing our society. It defines the agenda for this book.

There are no children for whom life runs completely smoothly, and there are many problems such as family break-up, commercial pressures and exam stress that affect children in all social classes. So our report is perhaps unusual in that much of it deals with the experiences of *children in general* rather than the problems of specific disadvantaged groups. The reason is simple. We think that the world in which most children grow up is more difficult than it should be. They experience the world as tough because it contains too much conflict and excessive competition – all the products of overblown individualism. Better values would benefit all.

The report is also different in another way. What follows is *based on evidence*, which makes it much more useful than simple assertion. It draws mainly on research evidence, some of it stronger than others, and also on surveys of adults and children by The Children's Society and on evidence submitted to The Good Childhood Inquiry by thousands of children and adults. Before the report was written, this evidence was reviewed and assessed chapter by chapter by the relevant experts on the inquiry panel and their papers are available on The Children's Society's Internet site.[17] These papers cover many more issues than the report, which concentrates on key issues of central importance to most families. There are, of course, all too many children in our society who face particular disadvantages, whether as a result of their ethnic background, because they have experienced abuse or trauma, or because, day-to-day, they live with the immense challenges imposed by serious illness or disability.

We could not hope to do justice to their specific needs in a short book of this kind (and we know that some of them have been well discussed elsewhere).[18] Instead, we have chosen to focus on just four specific groups – those with mental health difficulties, those who are 'looked after' by the state, those in custody and those in poverty. Nor do we deal at all with the physical care of children.

In interpreting the evidence, the panel of course used its own judgement. Some of our proposals are in line with the government's ambitious Children's Plan.[19] But many go beyond it and are addressed to parents, teachers, media and society at large, as much as they are to the government.

There is only one assertion that requires no evidence. Children are a sacred trust. They are not just our future adults. Their current feelings and experience matter as much as those of adults, and, being more vulnerable, they deserve even more consideration. Unless we care properly for our children, we shall never build a better world.

2. Family

*It's just a family that loves each other, and as long
as they do that's a happy family.*
(8-year-old girl)

*Well you can't really stop people having children if they want, but they
should be able to keep you happy and secure.*
(14-year-old girl)

Life begins in the family, and from a child's point of view
a loving family is the key to a good start in life. Families
vary greatly in their structure but the principles of loving
care are the same in any family and any culture – good
physical care, unconditional love and clear boundaries for
behaviour.

However, the context in which families live today in
Britain is in many ways quite new, and this raises new
challenges. Compared with a century ago, two changes
stand out. First, most women now work outside the home
and have careers, as well as being mothers. In Britain
70 per cent of mothers of 9 to 12-month-old babies now
do some paid work. This compares with only 25 per cent
twenty-five years ago – a massive change in our way of

life.[20] Meantime, the children are cared for by someone other than their parents.

The second change is the rise in family break-up. Women's new economic independence contributes to this rise: it has made women much less dependent on their male partner, as has the advent of the welfare state. As a result of increased break-up, a third of our 16-year-olds now live apart from their biological father; in the US it is a half.[21]

What do these major social changes mean for children? In much of this chapter we shall examine the effects on children of non-parental childcare, and the results of family break-up. But first we need to look at the basic needs of every child.

Love and Attachment

Children need above all to be loved. Unless they are loved they will not feel good about themselves, and will in turn find it difficult to love others. The basic need is for an enduring emotional tie to at least one specific person. Fifty years ago John Bowlby identified this as a core feature of early development and his insight has in many ways stood the test of time.[22] Attachment grows from the interaction between parental love and the response of babies to their parents.[23] It requires high levels of warmth from parent or caregiver, and sensitivity in their responses to the baby's needs. This style of parenting does not mean no routine – but, rather, a routine based on a sympathetic understanding of how the child feels inside. This is part of the law of love.

Some children never experience this type of affection. Many children have to be cared for by the state and often experience frequent changes of foster parents or of carers in children's homes. They deserve better and we discuss this in Chapter 8.

Parenting Styles

What is needed is unconditional love of children as people. But this is not the same as accepting whatever they do. Some parenting styles are more positive and successful than others. There are two dimensions that matter: one is the dimension of warmth versus lack of warmth, the second that of control versus lack of control.[24] This makes for four main styles of parenting, as shown in this figure.

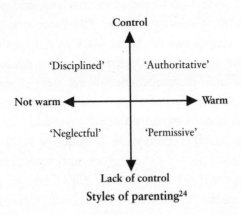

Styles of parenting[24]

Researchers have studied the effects of each style of parenting upon the way in which children develop. They agree that the style of parenting that is *loving* and yet *firm* – now known in the jargon as *authoritative* – is the most effective in terms of children's outcomes and well-being. In this approach boundaries are explained, in the context of a warm, loving relationship. The aim is not to secure compliance by fear. Children eventually internalize the parent's response, and act so as to please their own 'better selves'.

There are of course striking individual differences between children – even within the same family – in how easy or difficult they are. Every parent who has more than one child knows this. Some of these differences are genetic, some are linked to earlier experiences.[25] They are evident from birth onwards.

As they move into their second year, children's social relationships grow to include not only their parents but other family members, friends and familiar others. The security of their attachments within the family increases their expectations of love from others – and the ease with which they can care for others, and can in turn be cared for themselves. Children also fare better if their parents are consistent in how they interact with each other and with their children, and if they feel comfortable in talking with them about their feelings.[26]

Fathers

There is now increasing interest in the role of fathers. Fathers are no less important than mothers in a child's life. The closeness of fathers to their children influences the children's later psychological well-being, even after allowing for the mother's influence.[27] If fathers are more closely involved with their children, other things being equal, children develop better friendships, more empathy, higher self-esteem, better life satisfaction, and higher educational achievement. And they are less likely to become involved with crime or substance abuse. In contrast, if children are in conflict with their fathers or find them harsh or neglectful, they are much more likely to become destructive and aggressive themselves. Children whose fathers are bullies are much more likely to become bullies. Similarly, adolescent children whose fathers are anti-social or substance-abusers are much more likely to develop behavioural difficulties and aggression themselves.[28]

So in today's world are fathers becoming relatively more involved in caring for their children? There is indeed evidence of a culture shift towards greater male domesticity in Britain, continental Europe and the US[29] – though, even when the mother is working, fathers still do less with the children than mothers do. The sharpest increase in fathers' parenting activities is before the children are of school-age, when fathers are now expected to be nurturing and accessible as well as economically supportive.[30]

The more both fathers and mothers converse with their children and the better they set limits, the better the children do in school.[31] The impact of fathers shows up especially in adolescence. For example, in a classic German study, the children's relationship with their fathers while they were toddlers predicted their sense of self-worth as teenagers.[32] And the child's outcome at secondary school is linked especially to the father's input.[33] If we follow teenagers on into adult life, one study finds that their well-being as adults is more closely associated with their teenage relationship with their father than with their mother.[34]

Of course fathers are more likely to be involved with their children if mothers are also highly involved with the children; if the father's relationship with the mother is good; and if the father got involved with the child's life early on.[35] All family relationships are inter-related and it is wrong to single out individual relationships as uniquely important.

Working Parents

So what if both parents work? In a Children's Society survey adults were asked whether 'nowadays parents aren't able to spend enough time with their children'.[36] Sixty per cent agreed and only 22 per cent disagreed strongly. They were also asked whether 'these days more and more parents have to put their career first, even if this affects their family life'. Nearly half agreed.

So what is the effect of childcare when parents both work? This has been the subject of a major academic debate. Large-scale studies have traced children over a number of years to see how they fared,[37] and some concern has been raised.[38]

These studies have looked at the effects of being in childcare on both the cognitive development of the children (IQ, language and the like) and also on their happiness and well-being. On cognitive development the picture is reasonably clear. If children are put in group childcare before the age of 18 months, this has negligible effects one way or the other for most children. By contrast, beyond the age of 2 group care can lead to more rapid cognitive development, especially for children from disadvantaged backgrounds. The positive impact on cognitive development and academic skills is greatest where the childcare provided is of good quality and where the children come from a mixture of backgrounds.[39] Several major studies in the US report similar findings to those in Britain. In Britain the most substantial study finds positive benefits from pre-school education, both before the child goes to school and later on in Key Stage 1.[40]

But academic achievement is not all that matters. For most parents a key question is: 'What will being at nursery do for my child's happiness and well-being?' The results here are a little less clear-cut. When they reach school, some children who have had more group care are found to be more gregarious.[41] But some research suggests that children who have experienced long hours of nursery care are also somewhat more anti-social and aggressive; this has been found in the US. However, in the UK a large national study found that an early tendency towards anti-social behaviour by children who had experienced long hours of childcare had disappeared by age 11. One other UK study found a negative effect of long hours in early childcare when children were 6/7, but only for children with more advantaged backgrounds. So the findings are mixed in this country and further research is needed.[42] On top of this, some research indicates that children who have been in group care may encourage aggressive behaviour in other children. Among American 5-year-olds in kindergartens the level of aggression the children show depends not only on how long the children have been in group care themselves, but even more on how much group childcare the other children in the class have had.[43]

Group care is not of course the only kind of non-parental care for children. Children can be cared for by their grandparents, other relatives, child-minders or in small parent-run playgroups. In the Avon Longitudinal Study of Parents and Children (ALSPAC) it was found that, while mothers worked, 44 per cent of their babies were looked after by relatives, at least in part.[44] With this kind of care children develop very similarly to the ways they would have done if cared for by their parents – both in terms of cognitive and emotional development.

Having said all this, the development of a child depends much more on the quality of the relationship with the parents than on whether both parents work. Crucial are the warmth, understanding, interest and firmness which parents bring to the relationship with their child.[45]

Family Discord

It is also crucial how the parents get on with each other. It is remarkable how many parents do not realize how important this is for their children. In a British survey, teenagers and parents were asked whether they agreed with the statement: 'Parents getting on well is one of the most important factors in raising happy children.' Seven in ten of the teenagers agreed, but only a third of the parents did so.[46]

The teenagers are more right than the parents, as the research shows. Parental conflict and separation can have a disastrous effect on children, even though some children survive unscathed. The impact on the child of separation can be seen as early as the age of 3. The table shows some striking findings from the recent British study of children born at the beginning of the new millennium.[47] They reveal the difference in cognitive development and in behavioural difficulties between children growing up in different family situations. These differences are partly, but not wholly, due to more poverty and more mental health difficulties in lone-parent and step-parent families.

When their parents separate, children experience feelings of confusion, sadness and betrayal. But beyond this initial reaction, do children suffer long-term psychological difficulties? From over ninety studies we know that, on average, 50 per cent more children with separated parents have problems than those whose parents have not separated. This is true of a wide range of outcomes: academic

Percentage of children in each group having difficulties (3-year-olds)[47]

Children living with	Poor conceptual development	Behavioural difficulties
Married parents	9	5
Cohabiting parents	13	10
Lone parent	19	15
Step-parent	23	15

achievement, self-esteem, popularity with other children, behavioural difficulties, anxiety and depression.[48]

These are average results and not all children are affected equally – parental separation affects some children but not all.[49] Many of the problems dissipate over time: for instance, behavioural difficulties drop to normal levels by two years after parental separation. A recent overview of long-term effects concluded that the *majority* of children (at least two-thirds) appeared to be developing without psychosocial scars.[50] But of course the experience will be very different according to when the split between the parents occurred, how well the relationship between child and father continues, how close child and father are, and how far the mother and father are able to communicate with one another after the separation.

Should parents always stay together, if the children's welfare is their main consideration? Not if the level of conflict between the parents is very bad. The research shows that in such cases it is better for the parents to separate.[51] Interestingly, in families that break up, 50 per cent of the subsequent behavioural difficulties the children show were already visible years before the parents separated.[52] This illustrates the crucial importance of avoiding serious conflict between parents.

After a separation, the issue of conflict remains central. It is crucial how well the separated parents get on and communicate with each other. On average, children are less likely to become depressed or aggressive the better their parents are getting on, and the more they themselves see their separated father.[53] The children's relationships with their non-resident father are much better if there is good communication and contact between mother and father – as well as good relationships between the mother and the children.[54] The contact between separated fathers and their children often changes over time, and many fathers gradually drift back into contact after the initial separation from the mother.[55] Most children hate the loss of contact with their fathers and often experience substantial distress, anger or self-doubt as a result.

So it is a real worry that in Britain around 28 per cent of all children whose parents have separated have no contact with their fathers three years after the separation,[56] and in the US half of all children with separated parents have lost touch with their father within ten years. But there has to be a reservation here depending on the personality of the father: one study shows that if fathers have anti-social personalities, their children do better after the parental separation if there is no contact.[57]

If their parents are not getting on, many children turn

to their grandparents or other relations, if they are around. Grandparents' support can make a big difference to how well children cope with their parents' separation. Here in the table is what children said when asked who they confided in when their parents split up.[58] A high percentage of children reported that they did not talk intimately to anyone about their concerns, but those who did so were most likely to talk to their grandparents. And this contact with grandparents makes a big difference in reducing the adverse effect of bad events on the children's subsequent adjustment.[59] With today's geographical mobility, fewer parents live near grandparents[60] and community networks are weaker, providing a less supportive network of family and friends.

Who did children confide in intimately about their concerns in the first weeks after their parents split up? (Reports of children aged 9, %.)[58]

Grandparents/relations	14
Friends	12
Mother	10
Father	3
Brother or sister	3
Teacher	2
No one named	56

Once separated, what difference does it make if the parents set up with new partners? The answer is, on average, little difference: children who are in a lone-parent family *or* in a step-family are equally likely to have adjustment problems, when compared with children growing up with both their parents together.[61] If there is a stepfather, it is of course crucial how the mother and stepfather are getting along. If they are getting along, the children are likely to be all right.

But what makes parental separation such a disadvantage? Three main factors are at work. One is economic – you are poorer. Some studies say that this accounts for half the total effect, others much less.[62]

The second is problems in the parent–child relationship – linked probably to the experience of stress, low morale and depressive mood in both mothers and fathers. The table shows the striking prevalence of depression among mothers who were living apart from the father of their child.[63]

Percentage of mothers depressed when child is 5[63]	
Married parents	10
Cohabiting parents	15
Step-parent	19
Lone parent	23

The third factor is the experience of conflict. We have already seen how the scale of conflict between parents makes such a difference to children's outcomes – both the conflict between parents and any conflicts with a step-parent.[64]

Trends

If parental separation matters, how common is it? At present, about 15 per cent of mothers who give birth are already living on their own, 25 per cent are cohabiting, and 60 per cent are married. But, as we have seen, by age 16 a third of our children are living apart from their biological fathers. On present trends this figure will continue to rise, for many reasons. More parents are cohabiting rather than marrying, and cohabiting parents are more likely to split up.[65] Moreover, there is robust evidence for all European nations that children who experience parental divorce or separation are in their turn more likely to become divorced or separated.[66] This suggests that, as parental separation echoes through to the next generation, more and more children will experience it.

Some people argue that we should not worry about the trends in family break-up, because it enables people to escape from conflict. Would it were so simple! The sad fact is that in both Britain and the US those people who remain married are increasingly dissatisfied with their marriages.[67] So the key question is: how can we reduce the level of conflict in family life?

Nothing is more important for children than this. If parents gave more priority to maintaining their feelings for each other, this would do more for children than much of the rest of what they do for their children. If parents are separated, their continuing communication with each other – especially about the children – is crucial to how well the children fare.

RECOMMENDATIONS

Against the background of this analysis, we can now develop some proposals for promoting a better and more loving family life for our children.

The couple's commitment

A child needs parents who love the child and love each other. Child-rearing is one of the most challenging tasks in life and ideally it requires two people.[68] In addition, children learn to love through seeing the love between two adults. Though some children thrive despite family break-up, continuity in parenting is generally crucial for the development of inner security.

It follows that, when they have a child, the parents should have a long-term commitment to each other as well as to the welfare of the child.

Parenting education

Before a child is born, the parents should be fully in-formed of what is involved in bringing up a child – not only the physical demands and sacrifices, but the emotional demands and the stresses as well as the joys which it will bring to their own relationship. The NHS should ensure that parenting classes are available free to all parents around the birth of a child, especially their first.[69] Fathers as well as mothers should be encouraged to take courses in 'understanding your child', and be prepared for the strain of sleepless nights, inconsolable crying and financial pressure.

It is also important that people get this information while they are in school, before conception becomes an issue. So as part of 'personal and social education', young people should receive proper and culturally sensitive education in the skills of parenting and relationships, and in the process of child development – a subject of profound interest to many young people.

A civil birth ceremony

The birth of a child is a great event, and great events call for ceremonies and ritual. As with a wedding, a birth is an occasion to celebrate but also an occasion to express love and commitment in the presence of friends and relations and society at large. Traditionally in Britain, the christening has performed this type of function, and at present roughly one-third of children get christened or receive a birth ceremony in another religious faith. For children who do not get christened or experience another religious ceremony, a well-designed civil ceremony would reinforce the sense of commitment of parents and their resolve to do the best for their child, through a suitable vow made in public. The ceremony would be performed by the local Registrar, using a ritual similar to a civil marriage and would be celebrated in the Register Office or elsewhere and recorded in a certificate. It would normally happen when the child is between 6 and 12 months.

A similar facility is already available for a fee and used on a small scale in some places, but it would be valuable if it became a standard experience. Thus, when the child's birth was registered, the Registrar would simply arrange the date with the parents, for those who didn't want a religious ceremony.[70] The ceremony would be voluntary but free, reflecting the community's interest in welcoming the child into society.

Authoritative parenting

The evidence suggests that the best parenting includes unconditional love but also firmness in setting boundaries – what is sometimes called authoritative parenting. Parents should always give reasons and avoid physical punishments.

Children and working parents

Then there is the issue of whether both parents should work. The choice of staying at home should become more easily available. Thus parents should be entitled to leave, with guaranteed return to work, lasting for up to three years between the parents (as in France and Germany) – even if it is unpaid.[71] It should entail no loss of job security. At the same time, for parents who are both at work, there is an urgent need for higher-quality childcare.[72] Research has consistently shown the link between high-quality pre-school provision and good child outcomes at later ages. This requires well-educated staff who are well paid. The facilities should include outdoor space. Moreover, employers need to be more receptive when fathers, as well as mothers, request flexible working hours. We want a society where men can actively spend more time with their children. The value of flexible working with job security must be recognized.

Children with emotional or behavioural difficulties

If a child is clearly disturbed, local authorities should ensure that the parents have ready access to help and support. As we discuss in Chapter 7, there are good parenting programmes which can make a big difference, and if children are more seriously disturbed they should quickly receive help from the Child and Adolescent Mental Health Service.

Parental conflict

It is extremely important for children that their parents live in harmony with each other. If parents are in conflict, children should tell them how this impacts on them. All parents with these problems should have free access to psychological support to help them stay together or, if necessary, to help them manage to separate in a way that does least damage to the children.

If parents split up, children's voices must be heard and

taken into account in any decision about how they spend their time. Children in separated families fare best when they have close contact with each of their parents and all the important adults in their lives, including grandparents, aunts and uncles, cousins and family friends. And co-parenting by both mother and father should be the norm, except when issues of safety are involved.[73] Separating parents should always explain to the children what is happening, and the reasons for it.

We need above all to reverse the increase in family conflict. This is the heartache which damages so many children, however well they are otherwise brought up. As one 14-year-old from Manchester put it to us: 'I think all kids should have the right to live in a happy place where they feel safe and loved. I haven't felt like that in some time but I know my parents don't mean it. It's just they argue and take it out on me.'

3. Friends

You can't have a good childhood without friends every child needs friends.
(girl from Loughborough)

I sometimes get bullied because of my hair colour because it is ginger.
I sometimes feel all alone like I am trapped and like knoone cares.
(12-year-old girl)

As they grow older, children spend less and less time with their parents and more with other children – as the graph overleaf shows.[74] They are joining the wider human family. This is a crucial time. If they can develop good friendships at this stage, they are on their way to happy and fulfilled lives. When we asked children about the elements of a good childhood, friends was one of the words that they mentioned most often.[75]

So how are our children doing? Genetics is part of the story contributing to children's ability to make friends early.[76] But society has a huge influence and at present the trends are disappointing. Between 1986 and 2006 there was a drop in the number of 16-year-olds who said they had a best friend they could really trust – from 87 per cent to 82 per cent, a trend that was evident for both boys and girls.[77]

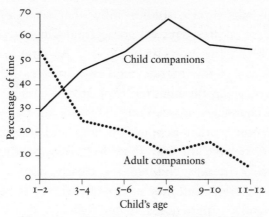

Time spent with adults and with other children[74]

So let us see how children form their friendships, and how this is the seedbed for developing habits of kindness and fairness. We can then look at children's need for places and spaces where they can play and develop together. Then we come to relationships between young men and women; and finally we look at the negative aspects of children's friendships – bullying and early criminal behaviour.

Friendship

Friendship begins early. By their second year children can often understand what upsets other children, and will go over to comfort them, even if they do not know them. The roots of empathy develop young. Even in their second year children become attached to other individual

35

children, and careful studies show that some children in day-care centres have on-going friendships, over half of which last for more than a year.[78] As time goes on, the play of young friends regularly involves 'pretend' situations, when the children explicitly discuss what the pretend characters are thinking. This is a key pathway to understanding other people's feelings and intentions – why they behave the way they do.[79] Because they care about their friends, children see clearly how a friend may be suffering, and they understand the links between their friend's experience and her feelings. The child is now an active participant in society, reading the minds of others.

Children's pleasure and excitement, their exuberant joy when playing with a friend, is clear. And children who make friends early do better later. They have greater moral sensibility and better understanding of social relationships.[80] They are also more popular, less bullied and less aggressive.[81] Children without friends feel lonely and are more likely to become depressed adults.[82] When children have a friend who moves away, they suffer, even as preschoolers: nightmares increase, and physiological tests show that their levels of anxiety increase.[83] If they are adolescent, they are more likely to become depressed.[84] Importantly, there is evidence that friends can buffer children from stressful changes in their lives, such as the arrival of a sibling or starting school.[85] Children who start primary school with a friend in their class adjust more easily and happily to the demands of the school day. As the years go by, having friends remains crucial to good adjustment to school.[86] And friends provide important protection when children are bullied.

So what can adults do to promote friendship? The main thing is love and good, helpful guidance on how to get along with someone, if a child is having difficulty with another child. Many parents also try to influence which children become their children's friends. In a classic study in Nottingham in the 1970s, 72 per cent of mothers of 7-year-olds said they would take action to restrict their child's friendship if they were not happy with it.[87] But, once children are playing, parents should keep a discreet distance – as psychologists have found, the creative imaginative play which is a core feature of friends' play stops once the parents turn up.[88] It is a private realm of fantasy that parents are rarely part of.

Unfortunately, some children are unpopular, and this has a major effect on their well-being: many children who are rejected by their peers will tend to become either aggressive or depressed.[89] If rejected by most other children, they will tend to associate with children who are (like them) more aggressive and reinforce the aggression in those who join them. All children are profoundly influenced by their peers – for good or ill.

Free-ranging Children[90]

Friendship is about exploring a world outside the family. For children to flourish they must have that freedom and it must include some physical freedom to range. But parents are increasingly anxious about letting their children play unsupervised. A survey of a representative sample of UK adults brought this out sharply.[91] They were asked: 'From what age should children be allowed to go out with their friends unsupervised?' They were then asked from what age they themselves had been allowed to do so. The table shows the contrast. Of the adults 39 per cent went out unsupervised before their 11th birthday, but only 17 per cent think today's children should do so. Similarly, in 1971 80 per cent of children aged 7–8 years went to school on their own, but by 1990 this had dropped to less than 10 per cent.[92]

There are various reasons for these changes, including two bad reasons: the car is there (so why not use it), and parents fear the abduction or murder of their child. But such hazardous events are incredibly rare, and the number of children murdered by strangers has been around its current level for decades.[93] The Home Office figures in the table opposite show that the risks here are tiny,[94] compared

Going out on your own (adults' replies, %)[91]		
	At what age should children go out with friends unsupervised?	At what age did you first go out with friends unsupervised?
Under 8	3	16
8–10	14	23
11–13	36	27
14+	43	32

with other risks faced by children, including risks from family members. Murders of children by strangers average around eleven a year, and most are of children over 11. The annual risk of murder by a stranger is one per million and of abduction six per million, which compares with twenty-four per million children who die each year on the roads and 2,400 per million who are injured in a road accident.[95] The problem is that television and newspapers now bring us the minutest visual details of every tragic murder, so that murders are now much more salient in people's minds. We need to restore a sense of balance.

What is true is that there are fewer places where children can play safely. There are fewer open spaces, and the roads are dangerous. We can encourage parents to be less risk averse, but we should also insist that planners provide a more child-friendly environment. In the 1970s Denmark had the worst child pedestrian casualty record in Europe. In 1976 the Danish government passed a law that forced local authorities to protect children from the

Murders of children under 16[94]						
Murdered by	2001/2	2002/3	2003/4	2004/5	2005/6	2006/7
Stranger*	6	17	14	7	13	11
Parent	40	52	34	29	24	33
Other family/ friend/acquaintance	9	10	12	11	11	9
No current suspect	7	14	12	11	4	15
Total	**62**	**93**	**72**	**58**	**52**	**68**

* Stranger includes relationship not known

dangers of motorized traffic on the way to and from school. Today Denmark has much higher levels of walking and cycling than the UK, and lower casualty rates.[96]

We can hardly be surprised when our children become obese, if we build over our open spaces in towns and our playing fields. This madness needs reversing and the British government's latest Children's Plan offers the hope of more play spaces and some reclaiming of the streets for children to play in.[97] It is important that its message gets through.

There is also today serious effort to make sure that organized sport is a major activity in schools – for all children, not just the most talented.[98] Organized team games, played together, are the foundation for many enduring friendships – as well as for physical health. Children delight in running around. Our bodies are made for that, and if we do not do enough of it, we are unlikely to flourish in body or in soul.

Children also need places indoors where they can congregate without their parents. For teenagers a youth club is a natural place – if it exists. But in Britain very many youth clubs closed their doors in the 1980s owing to lack of government support. Those who lost out were the most disadvantaged. It is difficult to think of any more short-sighted policy and the consequences are now apparent everywhere. If youngsters have 'nowhere to go', as 80 per cent of them complain,[99] they will go to street corners, which the government also dislikes.

Currently there are just over 11,000 youth clubs of all kinds in England, providing for 1.2 million 11 to

16-year-olds. This compares with a total number of 4.5 million children within this age group across the country – so only 1 in 4 has access to a youth club. Even where clubs do exist, young people say that the opening times and range of activities and services on offer at most youth clubs do not meet their needs.[100] In a recent Audit Commission poll of adults on the issue of what most needed improving in their local area, more people (43 per cent) mentioned activities for teenagers rather than any other topic.[101] Current plans for an extended school day ('extended schools') are excellent. But they do not remove the need for more grown-up leisure facilities outside school.

Some studies in the UK and Norway find poor outcomes for young people who visit youth centres – but these are related to the 'old-style' youth clubs that provide little more than a place to go and lack structure or activities. In contrast, the recent Make Space Youth Review sponsored by 4Children proposes structured activities such as programmes of art, games, sport and music with specialist classes organized by inspirational adults. Participation in these has been found to lead to positive outcomes.[102]

Children also need plenty of open space, including the ability to mix with adults in town centres. We utterly oppose attempts to establish no-go areas for children. And free bus travel for children can greatly help to establish their independence and ability to explore: it already exists in London and some other places.

Romance and Sex

Until children reach puberty, most friendships are between children of the same sex. From puberty onwards heterosexual friendships become increasingly common, and important to young people. During the teenage years, romantic thoughts about others (which can start early in childhood) become nearly universal; these romantic ideas and feelings increasingly turn into romantic relationships. For young people with a boyfriend or girlfriend, and for those without, romantic thoughts, discussions and experiences are an important feature of their lives.

There is relatively little systematic research on these romantic relationships in Britain, so we have to look to the US for information. There, about 25 per cent of 12-year-olds report having had a romantic relationship in the previous eighteen months. This rises to 50 per cent of 15-year-olds, and 70 per cent of 18-year-olds.[103] The first foray into romantic relationships can be a journey into new emotional terrain, marked by new and intense feelings such as love, lust, jealousy and loss. Such intense emotions can lead to psychological difficulties.[104] Early involvement in romantic relationships has been associated with a cluster of problem areas – alcohol and drug use, school difficulties and delinquency. We also know that romantic relationships can be linked to positive developments, such as feelings of self-worth and positive self-esteem.

In Britain and most Western countries there has been a dramatic fall in the age at which people have their first sexual experience (see table below).[105] The reason for this is not biological: contrary to popular belief the average age of first menstruation for girls has remained at 13½ for the last half century.[106] So earlier sex is not in that sense inevitable. It is the product of many forces – more privacy when both parents work, more contraception, commercial pressures towards premature sexualization, and fundamental changes of attitude – by 1994 virtually all young men and women had their first sexual experience without being married.[107]

Age at first full sexual intercourse (median age)[105]			
		Men	Women
Young people aged 20 in	1953	20	21
	1963	18	19
	1991	17	17
	1998	17	16

The key issue is what has happened to the relation between sex and love? The figures don't fit a romantic account.[108] Teenage sex for boys in Britain is more a matter of physical attraction and of peer pressure than of love and commitment. Many girls who have early sex regret it quite soon[109] and only a half of our young people use contraception when they first make love. Not surprisingly, there are some babies. Having a baby in the teenage years is higher in the UK than in any other country in Western Europe, but not as high as in the USA. The prospects for these babies are well below average. This is so in every dimension – they do less well at school, and they are more likely to have mental health difficulties as children and as adults. Having children while still a teenager is also not great for most of the mothers – it can be bad emotionally, and bad for their chances of getting a satisfying job.[110]

It is interesting to contrast the British situation with that in Holland. Things are very different there – with more links between love and sex, more use of contraception, and fewer babies (see table below). The teenage fertility rate in Britain is 27 per 1,000 women aged 15–19, compared with 5 per 1,000 in the Netherlands.[111] One plausible explanation is the more open attitude of Dutch parents and the fact that sex education there begins in primary school. Though Dutch teenagers begin sex at about the same age as in Britain, for them sex is much

First experience of teenage sex[111]						
	UK			Holland		
	Boys	Both	Girls	Boys	Both	Girls
% saying main reason was love and commitment to relationship	14		47	56		58
% saying a main reason was physical attraction	47		35	17		13
% who discussed it with their mothers		23			50	
% who used contraception		50			85	

more closely associated with love than it is here, and many fewer babies are born to young people. There are surely lessons from this.

Bullying and Criminal Behaviour

We turn now to the darker side of children's relationships with each other. Some children bully, especially those who are rejected by their peers. It is not good for the bulliers, and it is not good for those who get bullied. Bullying can involve repeated physical attack by one or more bigger children, or repeated psychological attack – name-calling, rumour-spreading, ostentatious exclusion. Physical bullying is more common among boys, and psychological bullying among girls. Most bullying occurs in school, but some happens on the way to school and back. It is not confined to big cities.

About 12 per cent of children aged 10–14 say that they have been bullied more than once or twice in the previous six months.[112] The evidence suggests that this has not increased since 2002.[113] But there is also a new form of harassment, cyber-bullying, which is even nastier because the bully remains anonymous and the bullying is in public. A bully can now spread malicious stories or pictures about someone far and wide through mobile phones or the Internet, without being identified. This is on the rise and 7 per cent of schoolchildren aged 11 to 13 say they have received nasty or threatening text messages or e-mails, at least once in a while.[114]

Rates of bullying seem to be similar in many advanced countries:[115] Britain and the USA are no worse than elsewhere. But every country needs to improve. Schools can do a lot. Clearly, every school should have an anti-bullying policy, and teachers should be trained in recognizing and eradicating bullying. In many cases peer support groups can work quite well, where victims can approach named individuals for help and support. An international survey of twelve different interventions showed an average reduction of bullying by 12 per cent.[116] The most important factor accounting for a child stopping bullying is if he moves to a more pro-social group of friends.[117]

Not only do children get bullied; they are often victims of crime. In fact, children of 10–15 are more likely to be victims of crime than older children or adults (see figure).[118] In any twelve months a third of children of that age are victims of crime.

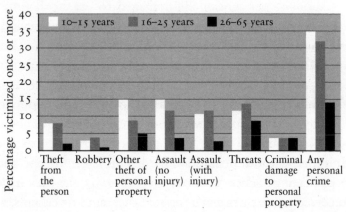

Percentage at each age who are victims of crime in any twelve months[118]

The majority of these crimes are inflicted by other children. For both young men and women the most common age for violent offences is 16. As many as 20 per cent of teenagers report committing a violent offence in the previous twelve months (see figure below).[119] These figures are disturbing. For decades they have been getting worse. Non-violent youth crime has now stabilized and begun to fall. But violence seems a major problem in our way of life.[120]

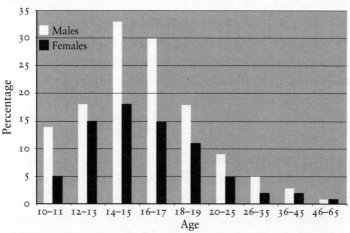

Percentage who committed a violent offence in last twelve months[119]

RECOMMENDATIONS

So how can we promote and support friendship, and encourage children to be kind and respectful to each other? Again, values will be crucial, as well as psychological help for disturbed and rejected children (see Chapters 5 and 7). But some other specific lessons emerge from this chapter.

Valuing friendship

Parents and teachers need to take children's friendships seriously. This means encouraging children to make friends, to play and study with friends and to invite them home. When the family considers moving, it should take into account the impact on the children's friendships. Children should wherever possible be helped to keep their friends, since they are a major source of strength. This applies when children start school, move school or move class.

Space for play and sport

Public authorities should give high priority to open spaces where children can play unsupervised. They need not only playgrounds but also places where they can explore. And they need playing fields for regular sport. All new housing developments and all new schools should include proper space for play. And no open play space, recreation area or playing field should be built on, unless equivalent open space for children is provided elsewhere. We also applaud all efforts to reclaim the streets for children.

Youth centres

There should be at least one really high-quality Young People's Centre, separate from school, for every 5,000 teenagers.[121] This should offer attractive and interesting activities (like music, dance, drama, art, IT, sport and games and volunteering) – as well as mentoring, psychological support and careers advice.[122] There must be more professional support for young people in a non-school setting offering a 'different', adult atmosphere. The proposal should be carefully piloted.

Bullying

Every school should have a state-of-the-art bullying policy,[123] with an annual report on the incidence of bullying. Equally important, all teachers should receive explicit training in how to recognize and prevent bullying. As one generous-hearted child said, 'Schools should help the bully by talking to them and finding out why they're unhappy and why they bully.'

Sex and relationships education

Sex education should not be taught as biology. It should be part of relationships education, with the biological element placed within the context of shared experience between equal partners. As sex can create human beings, sex and relationships education should be treated with seriousness and it should centre on love and responsibility within the context of family life.[124] The evidence is that when this is done (as in Holland) early sex is more likely to occur between partners who know and care for each other, with fewer babies resulting. Such education should begin by age 11, and should be a statutory part of the Personal, Social and Health Education curriculum.

Good friendships are the foundation for a child's entry into the social world. But what kinds of lifestyle does this social world offer?

4. Lifestyle

When you've bought something you feel proud like it
releases a happy hormone.
(14-year-old girl)

Stop going to the pub's every night
No pubs! No pubs! No pubs!
(10-year-old girl)

By lifestyle we mean how children spend their leisure time, and what leisure activities really excite them. Compared with fifty years ago, there have been three massive changes in the world of children. First, they nearly all have more money. Second, they mostly have more leisure. And, third, the communications revolution has introduced a completely different set of activities which they can enjoy – from television to videogames, mobile phones and the Internet. The effect of all this is a quite new youth culture, more separate than ever from the world of adults.

Fifty years ago most young people left school at 15 and went to work. They had little money of their own, and gave much of what they earned to their parents: they lived throughout in a world dominated by adults – first

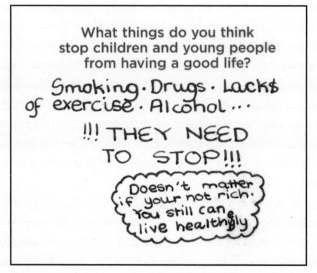

their parents and then their employers. Today by contrast most teenagers have money which they spend on themselves: there is now a massive teenage market.

Teenagers also have more leisure. More of them continue their education longer and fewer of those who have left education are in work. Young people spend much of their free time with people of their own age, and they are in many ways less dependent on adults. As deference of every kind has declined, so has the deference of teenagers to both parents and teachers.

Moreover the IT equipment which has brought so many blessings to their lives was unknown to many of their parents, and as a result for the first time in history most children are better at many tasks than their parents. This IT gives access to a whole media world of wealthy celebrities, pop stars and football heroes, which provides role models far removed from their own existence and from their parents' experience.

Thus the culture in which teenagers live is more different from that of their parents than ever before. It is not surprising that many adults are apprehensive. But is the apprehension justified, or are human beings so adaptable that we need not worry?

We have to be careful. Adults have always been uneasy about change. As *The Times* of London reported in 1816:

The indecent foreign dance called the *Waltz* was introduced . . . at the English Court on Friday last . . . It is quite sufficient to cast one's eyes on the voluptuous intertwining of the limbs, and close compressure of the bodies ... to see that it is far indeed removed from the modest reserve which has hitherto been considered distinctive of English females ... we feel it a duty to warn every parent against exposing his daughter to so fatal contagion.[125]

As we have seen, most children lead reasonably happy lives. They enjoy the good things which modern culture and technology brings. But modern culture also involves three serious dangers, as we shall show:

- It encourages the view that to be happy you have to be wealthy and beautiful.

  (Consumerism)

- It encourages a conflictual and often violent model of human relationships.

  (Aggression)

- It encourages physical inactivity, and eating, drinking and smoking to excess.

  (Unhealthy living)

All of these dangers are connected with the new communications technologies which so dominate the leisure time of children: television, CDs and DVDs, videogames, the Internet and mobile phones. These technologies have opened up wonderful new sources of knowledge, music, entertainment and friendship. Television and DVDs are somewhat passive but videogames require intensely focused activity. And the Internet is more mentally challenging than either. Mobiles, e-mails, texting and, now, web-sites make possible modes of friendship unknown before. These new technologies are a genuine blessing but they have also brought serious problems.

The context for all of this is how children spend their

How children spend their time over the year (2001) (average hours per week, including school holidays)[126]

	8–11	12–15	8–15
Television/Media	15.9	18.2	17.0
Computer use	3.3	4.4	3.9
Cinema etc.	1.9	3.7	2.8
Games/hobbies	11.3	4.5	7.9
Shopping	2.0	1.6	1.8
Sports/walking (non-school)	3.3	4.2	3.7
Social visits	3.0	3.8	3.4
Travel (not to school)	6.6	6.3	6.5
Conversation	0.6	1.5	1.0
Eating	8.0	7.6	7.8
Unpaid work	2.8	4.5	3.7
Paid work	0.3	1.0	0.7
Reading/homework	3.0	4.9	4.0
School (incl. travel)	26.1	27.7	26.9
Washing/dressing	5.7	5.7	5.7
Sleep	73.7	68.0	70.9
Other	0.6	0.6	0.6
Total	168.0	168.0	168.0

time. We know about this from a large diary study involving a representative sample of children aged 8–15 in 2001 – see table on page 55.[126] On average they spent seventeen hours a week watching television (as a primary activity). In addition they used the computer or played videogames for four hours a week – time which in 1975 was spent watching television.[127] Other games and hobbies took up another eight hours, and shopping two hours.

At the same time children have become major owners of consumer durables.[128] Eight in ten 5 to 16-year-olds have their own television, and seven in ten own a DVD player. Two thirds have their own mobile telephone, and seven in ten have Internet access.

But more important than their equipment, or the time for which they use it, is the content to which it gives access. This has opened up wonderful possibilities, but also dangers.

Consumerism

The first of these is a new form of consumerism. This emerges partly from the modern media of communications and mass marketing, which children experience daily. But on top of this, children now have an unprecedented purchasing power of their own, which brings into their world issues of consumer choice previously confined to adults.

Children's money comes partly from their own earnings, and partly from pocket money from their parents.

Though paid work by children has declined, nearly 40 per cent of all 15-year-olds have some regular job; it provides average weekly earnings of £16.50.[129] Teenagers also get pocket money, which provides roughly as much income as earnings do. Some 10 per cent of 15-year-olds are getting over £30 a week in income.

This amounts to substantial purchasing power. Each year in Britain children under 16 spend some £3 billion of their own money: £1 billion on clothes and shoes, £0.7 billion on snacks and sweets, £0.6 billion on music and CDs, and £0.6 billion on software and magazines. They can also put enormous pressure on their parents to buy things for them – what is known as pester power: the British children's clothing market alone is worth £6 billion a year.[130]

A growing market of this size has naturally attracted massive advertising. Brand loyalties get established early in life: by the age of two, children handle a new toy differently according to whether or not they have seen it on the television screen the previous day. By the age of three, they prefer an advertised brand to another which tastes just the same. It is not until they are 10–11 that they can identify the persuasive intent in an advertisement.[131] So it is not surprising that the advertising and marketing expenditure directed at children in the USA has soared to $15 billion, compared with virtually nothing twenty years ago.

Much advertising is good fun and is a proper part of marketing operations. After all, the aim of the advertiser is to make you buy his particular brand rather than someone else's. But the overall effect of advertising is to make people feel they need more in total than they otherwise would.[132] In a Children's Society survey adults were asked whether 'advertising to children at Christmas puts pressure on parents to spend more than they can really afford'.[133] Nine out of ten adults agreed. Most of this pressure comes through peer-group effects, since peers watch the same advertisements and become indirect promoters of the brands which are considered cool. Some advertisers explicitly exploit the mechanism of peer pressure, while painting parents as buffoons.[134] And many advertisements on the Internet are presented to look like regular media content.[135]

In its most extreme form advertising persuades children that 'You are what you own.' Some 34 per cent of 9 to 13-year-olds say they'd 'rather spend time buying things than almost anything else', and 45 per cent say 'the only kind of job that I want when I grow up is one that gives me a lot of money'.

Advertising is not of course the only problem. There is also the constant exposure in television soaps, drama and chat-shows to people who are richer and more beautiful than most of us. Children today know in intimate detail the lives of celebrities who are richer than they will ever be, and mostly better-looking. This exposure inevitably raises aspirations and reduces self-esteem.[136]

These celebrities become role models. When children are asked what they want to be in life, they frequently reply 'a celebrity'. But the private lives of many celebrities, as reported, are not particularly exemplary. And the way they are portrayed automatically encourages the excessive pursuit of wealth and beauty.

Effects of consumerism

So how does media-driven consumerism affect the overall well-being of children? Juliet Schor has done a major study of the effect of consumerism on the psychological well-being of 10 to 13-year-olds. She constructed a scale of Consumer Involvement, which measured how much the children cared about possessions, shopping, brands, money and the like. She also measured their use of television and other media. And finally she measured their relationship with their parents, and the level of their mental health. She claimed that the evidence supported the following story.[137] Other things being equal, the more a child is exposed to the media (television and Internet), the more materialistic she becomes; the worse she relates to her parents; and the worse her mental health.[138] And the effects of the media on children's attitudes are worse on poor children, who are already most at risk. Studies in Britain have come to similar conclusions.[139]

This section raises clear issues regarding child protection. The clearest issues are to do with advertising. While adults can be expected to use their own judgement, it is not acceptable for young people to be exposed to advertising which produces demonstrable harm. In Sweden television advertising directed at children under 12 is banned.[140]

Aggression

A second problem with modern mass communication is that much of its content is extremely violent – both on television and in videogames. On **television**, violence is frequently shown as a part of normal human life (not just a feature of crime or war). The violence is both physical and psychological, and violent argument appears as a standard response to disagreement. To be sure, there is plenty of violence in Shakespeare and in the cinema. But people used to go to the cinema once a week, whereas our children now watch television for an average of seventeen hours a week. The majority have a set in their bedroom, and many switch it on the moment they get home.

There is much evidence that exposure to violent images encourages aggressive behaviour.[141] First, there are standard experiments, where you expose children to violent films and they then behave more violently in the playground. Second, we can trace children as they grow, and we observe that those who watch more television end up more aggressive. Third, we can study whole communities. One remote Canadian town was unable to receive television until 1973; but, when television arrived, the children became more aggressive. So what happens on the television does have effects, and television remains the medium which children use more than any other.[142]

But **videogames** are another major feature of most children's lives. They are a lot of fun – often instructive, stimulating and frequently played with friends. But they are also a source of exposure to violence.[143] This is violence in which the individual has to engage himself in wounding others and it is more 'for real' than playing with toy guns or swords. The US Surgeon General has studied the factors which account for whether a child's behaviour is aggressive. In order of importance these are, first, gang membership, and second, playing violent videogames – followed well behind by parent–child relations, being male, exposure to television violence, having anti-social parents, low IQ, broken family, poverty and substance abuse.[144]

Then there is the **Internet** with all its wonderful potential for exploration and discovery – and of course danger. As well as covering the benefits, Tanya Byron's Review[145] covered these dangers at length and also included detailed proposals to make it easier for parents to influence how their children use the net.[146] She stressed in particular the dangers coming from exposure to sexual content designed for adults, and the 'stranger-danger' from children providing too much information about themselves. According to the review, 57 per cent of British 9 to 19-year-olds have come into contact with online pornography – 36 per cent by stumbling on it and 25 per cent by receiving it by unsolicited e-mail. These figures are similar to those elsewhere in Europe.[147] We have also mentioned the unpleasant use of the Internet for cyber-bullying.

Another new feature of life introduced by the Internet are the social networking sites such as today's MySpace and Facebook. Such sites are an endless source of fascination but they risk encouraging a commoditization of friendship where what counts is not the depth and quality of a friendship, but exactly how many 'friends' you can list on your page. Such sites also encourage the view that value is gained through relationships by exhibition – by detailing and publicizing every aspect of your life (in the best light you choose) – and the more people who are watching, the more legitimate a presence you are in your community.

But in our view the most dangerous aspect of media content is the lurch towards more and more violence, much of it designed to satisfy the adult market.[148] We know from controlled studies that exposure to violence can breed violence. So it seems likely that the upward trend in media violence is helping to produce the upward trend in violent behaviour – and also the growth of psychological conflict in family relationships.

Unhealthy Living

If our culture fosters consumerism and aggression, it is also in many ways unfavourable to physical health and well-being.

Alcohol

The biggest problem is alcohol. Most adults enjoy a drink and young people are no different. It is a regular feature of all Western societies. But what makes Britain different is the pattern of binge drinking engaged in by adolescents as well as younger adults. Among young people aged 16 to 19, a quarter engage in hazardous drinking, meaning 'an established pattern of drinking which brings the risk of physical and psychological harm now or in the future'.[149] This is based on their replies to questions, which also show that no less than 14 per cent are assessed as alcohol-dependent.

Much of this drinking starts well before 16. Of children aged 15, all but 6 per cent have had a drink, and have drunk at least once without their parents' knowledge.[150] Twenty per cent had got drunk in the week before being questioned,[151] and on a typical drinking day 45 per cent drink over the recommended daily limit of four units.[152]

This type of heavy drinking puts young people at risk in many ways. It encourages fights, fuels discord at home, increases accidents, and adds to the likelihood of unprotected sex. It increases the risk of alcohol addiction,[153] which is by far the most serious addiction in our community, affecting 7 per cent of adults, compared with only 1 per cent dependent on hard drugs.[154] And it brings serious risks of physical illness. Deaths from chronic liver disease and cirrhosis have more than doubled over the last forty years, while at the same time alcohol consumption has doubled.[155]

Some parents are able to socialize their children into a pattern of moderate drinking by the end of their teens. But the ease of access to cheap alcohol makes this difficult for most parents. And some parents are themselves obviously addicted – no less than 11 per cent of children live with a parent who misuses alcohol.[156]

What is needed is a change of attitude, especially to being drunk. Twenty-five years ago people would never have forecast the change in attitude to smoking that has happened nor the degree to which smoking is now regulated. A similar change is needed in relation to heavy drinking. In addition, the following practical measures could be considered.

- Higher taxes on alcohol. All the evidence shows that alcohol consumption is lower, the higher the price of alcohol relative to incomes. If higher taxes were introduced on alcohol, there would have to be compensating reductions elsewhere to protect the incomes of the poor.
- Restricted advertising of alcohol. A total advertising ban is now being discussed in Scotland. Or there could be a ban up to 9 p.m.
- Strict enforcement of the law on sales to under-age children.
- More Youth Centres where young people could develop constructive pursuits in an alcohol-free environment.
- Better education in schools about alcohol, smoking, healthy eating and drugs.

Illegal drugs

Although fewer young people's lives are affected by drugs than by alcohol, drugs are a major social problem in Britain. Hard drugs can have significant effects on life expectancy and on mental health. Cocaine and, especially, heroin, are highly addictive. And they reduce a person's ability to be a good parent – as many as 300,000 parents are dependent on hard drugs.[157]

Under 5 per cent of young people are dependent on hard drugs.[158] But cannabis use is of course far more common. Some 40 per cent of 16 to 19-year-olds have tried it. Among adolescents and some adults, cannabis is a part of the leisure culture for a significant part of the population, though most are occasional users. The risks of occasional use are uncertain but include reduced motivation and ability to concentrate, and in some tragic cases schizophrenia. In one review the rate of schizophrenia was 1.4 per cent among users, compared with 1.0 per cent among non-users.[159]

There is some evidence that cannabis use among teenagers has been slowly decreasing.[160] We are therefore concerned at the recent reclassification of cannabis from Class C to Class B, as this will effectively criminalize large numbers of adolescents with no evidence that it will reduce usage.

More generally, we are concerned at the degree to which the legal prohibition of the drug trade results in many young people, especially those on council estates, becoming caught up in crime. This makes it extremely difficult for parents to give their children a decent start in life. Consideration of drug policy should take into account the adverse effects of the drug trade on the lives of children and young people, and not only the effect of the drugs themselves.[161]

Obesity

Another major health problem is obesity. The problem is increasing. In 2006 17 per cent of 12 to 15-year-old boys in Britain were obese, compared with 11 per cent in 1995. For girls, the figure is 15 per cent, compared with 12 per cent a decade earlier.[162] Obese children are highly likely to become obese adults – 83 per cent of obese children aged 10 to 14 remain obese into adulthood.[163]

The chief medical officer has described increasing obesity in childhood as a 'time-bomb'. It looks set to become a major factor in life expectancy, and it already costs the health service more in medical costs than smoking does. If it continues to rise at the present rate, by 2023 there will be a 54 per cent increase in Type 2 diabetes and by 2051 life expectancy will be reduced by five years.[164]

Our weight is determined by how much exercise we take and by how much we eat. The most striking change in recent years has been the decline in exercise. In fact for adults the rise in obesity can be traced directly to a reduction in exercise – less exercise while working and doing housework, less exercise walking to work, and less sport.[165] For children there have been three huge changes over the last fifty years:

- Fewer children walk or bicycle to school.[166]
- Children play less sport.
- Children spend much more time sitting in front of the television, computer or playstation, rather than running around.[167]

We have already discussed the first two of these. But the third reflects a move from active to passive leisure which is very undesirable. Our bodies and our minds need active physical exercise, and our parents and teachers are failing if they do not provide it.

The chief medical officer's 2004 report stated that 'for children and young people, a total of at least 60 minutes of at least moderate-intensity physical activity each day is needed'. This excludes ordinary walking. It is a good objective, though a daily *average* of 60 minutes would be more realistic. At present only 56 per cent of 15-year-olds do exercise where they 'have to breathe harder and faster' on three or more days a week.[168]

The other side of the coin is unhealthy eating. For example, more than 60 per cent of children regularly eat crisps after school.[169] The National Diet and Nutrition Survey of 2000 showed that high proportions of 7 to 14-year-olds were failing to achieve healthy eating guidelines.[170]

The government's policy to reduce obesity in children is to provide information, to make healthy choices easier, and to legislate only if all else fails. So far, little has happened to improve spending patterns and there is every indication that the problem will become more serious. In 2004 the government was spending £7 million a year on advertising in favour of healthy eating, while the food industry was spending £743 million on advertising, in favour of unhealthy eating.[171]

In 2007 the media regulator Ofcom banned all advertisement of food that is high in fat, salt or sugars (HFSS) in or around television programmes of particular appeal to children. However, since the overwhelming majority of children's viewing time is outside of children's airtime, these restrictions can only have limited effect. For this reason, the British Medical Association, the Food Standards Authority and all four Children's Commissioners have expressed support for the removal of all HFSS food advertising before the 9 p.m. watershed.

Smoking

The fourth unhealthy practice is smoking. Too many young people find it necessary to smoke in order to relax, for example when they come out of school. For too many of them, especially those who have parents who smoke, smoking is still part of social life when they are with their friends.

In 2007 some 15 per cent of 15 to 16-year-olds were regular smokers, with a higher rate in working-class families.[172] There are more girl smokers than boys and they smoke more heavily, with a quarter of all girl smokers smoking over twenty-five cigarettes a week.

Smoking among children has been declining.[173] But as everyone now knows, smoking remains the single biggest cause of preventable illness and premature death in Britain. It is highly addictive, and two-thirds of adult smokers want to give it up but can't.[174] Public policy is making considerable inroads on the habit, through rises in price and restrictions on where you can smoke, and, it is hoped, this will continue.

RECOMMENDATIONS

So what can be done about these issues? We must start with a general point. Consumerism, aggression and unhealthy living all have their allure. But they are often unsatisfying. We all do a bit of them, but they only take root enough to harm us if we lack enough other projects or interests that engage us. Nature abhors a vacuum. If we have satisfying interests and pursuits, they fill the vacuum. If not, other things do and we fall prey to the commercial pressures that appeal to the weaker aspects of our nature.

This point is well illustrated by a recent article in the *British Medical Journal*.[175] The question posed is how to reduce unhealthy living (alcohol, etc.). The article shows that specific school policies targeted at each particular form of damaging behaviour had little sustained effect. What did more to reduce unhealthy living was a school ethos based on general principles of positive living – consideration for others, self-understanding and the cultivation of constructive interests.

That is why values are so important, and they are the subject of the next chapter. But there are also specific things that can be done to restrict the negative impact of commercial pressures on children.

Advertising to children

We should not hesitate to protect children when the danger is clear enough.[176] We do not allow sex shops next to schools, and nor should we allow commercial advertisements specifically aimed at children under 12. This is banned in Sweden, and they do not find it hard to define such advertising. But there is a difficulty in controlling advertisements beamed into the country from abroad. This suggests that a UK ban should apply to the company placing the advertisement, not to the platform carrying it, and that it should apply to all companies with marketing operations in Britain.

There is also the problem of unhealthy advertisements aimed at adults but seen by children. Thus we should also ban the television advertising before 9 p.m. of unhealthy foods (high fat, sugar and salt) and of alcohol.

Media understanding

We cannot control most of the violent material that appears on television, nor consumerist advertising to adults, nor distorted press reporting. But we can educate young people to adopt a critical attitude to what they see, hear and read. All secondary schools should teach the critical understanding of media as part of 'personal, social and health education'.

Alcohol

The surest way to discourage excessive alcohol consumption is to raise its price in relation to average incomes. Despite recent tax increases, alcohol needs to be taxed more heavily still, while at the same time other taxes are reduced so as to keep the overall tax burden on different income groups unchanged. Such a change in alcohol taxation will become possible if enough people talk about it, just as a sustained campaign produced the ban on smoking in public places.

Exercise

It is internationally accepted that children need at least seven hours of moderately intensive exercise every week (averaging at least one hour a day). This includes brisk walking, cycling, swimming, dancing and of course sport. Every parent and child should understand this and do their best to achieve it. (There must also be places to exercise – see Chapter 3.)

Most children enjoy their lives, and we should not worry if what they enjoy is different from what their parents enjoyed. But we should worry if their level of enjoyment is declining, and the evidence suggests that it is. That is why we need a radical rethink about values – the values of society and the values which children absorb.

5. Values

To be in a good school with good people because if they grow up around good people then they usually become good people.
(14-year-old girl from London)

When you are younger, you forget your values because you want to look cool or you want to belong, but as you get older, your values become more important.
(girl from Norwich)

Our values and beliefs are what we live by. They tell us how to behave in our dealings with others, and they give us our purposes in life. So they define both our morality and our aspirations. They represent our vision of the person we would like to be.

There are of course many values which most young people and their parents would agree to, if asked. We should 'do as we would be done by'. We should be fair, because everybody matters equally. We should not harm others, and we should be kind and helpful. We should have the courage of our convictions, and not follow the crowd. Giving is better than getting. And so on.

For centuries these values have been drawn from religious belief, or more recently from secular beliefs about social obligation. But overall there is now less confidence about values than used to be the case. And the values of generosity and fairness are much more difficult to inculcate when all parents, religious and non-religious, and their children are repeatedly told they need to possess more material goods for themselves and to compete successfully against others.

This void has left the way open to excessive individualism – the belief that things will work out all right if everybody looks after themselves. In consequence, as we have shown, most adults think that young people today are more selfish than the previous generation. If they are right, it helps to explain the troubling fact we began this report with – that more young people are unhappy than used to be the case.

For the philosophy behind excessive individualism is fundamentally flawed. A major finding of psychological research is that unselfish people become on average happier than people who are more preoccupied with themselves. Of course it sometimes hurts to behave unselfishly but on average being less selfish makes you happier. This finding is based not simply on interpersonal comparisons but also on experimental evidence over time.[177] It has the most profound consequences.

Clearly we should all benefit if other people were nicer to us. But what the research shows is that we ourselves benefit from being nicer to other people. This shows more clearly than ever the central importance for our society of the kind of people we are. If we want to improve our quality of life, we must above all produce better people.

By better people we mean those who are well adjusted to themselves, to their family and friends and to their wider social environment; people who have a sense of their personal identity and potential and who seek to realize their lives fully by seeking fulfilment in helping others. We want a society in which people observe the rights of others, including the rights of children embodied in the UN Convention on the Rights of the Child.

Such a society has to be built on the attitudes which people acquire in their childhood. So how do young people acquire a concern for others? Are there well-established ways in which parents and teachers can foster this concern? Is moral education old-fashioned and counter-productive, or is it in fact more necessary than ever when the media bombard our children daily with worries about their self-presentation and self-advancement? We believe it is more important now than ever to put children in touch with their better selves, and to help them handle the selfish streak that is in each of us.

How Children Acquire Morality

Children are born with a moral potential, which is in their genes to a greater or lesser degree – identical twins end up more similar in moral character than non-identical twins do.[178] This moral capacity is there in people because of its survival value.[179] But it only develops through fruitful human interaction, first with parents, then with other children, and then with other adults including teachers and pastors.

Without fruitful relationships, the spirit withers. Children who are abused rarely become altruistic or empathetic later on. What children need is unconditional love but also firm guidance about boundaries and how to behave. The right guidance is based on reason, not command – 'authoritative', not authoritarian.[180] And the main principles are rather simple:

- Other people matter as much as you do.
- So consider how your behaviour will affect them and how they will feel.
- Agreement is bound to involve compromise.

Such teaching would have little chance of success if it did not interact with ideas already latent in children. Even as young pre-schoolers, children are really interested in feelings – not just their own but those of others. As 3-year-olds they ask questions about why people do what they do, and why they feel what they feel. They love books in which the characters show emotions, and ask about them. Emotion is a central topic of interest among young friends.[181]

One can see moral ideas developing clearly in observational studies on 3-year-olds left alone in a room to sort out who should have which toy.[182] One child who has two toys is observed giving one of the toys to a child who has none. Or, alternatively, a third child is heard suggesting that this would be a fair thing to do. Hitting is disapproved of because 'How will she feel if you hit her?' Even quite young children can become quite skilled at the non-violent resolution of conflict – one of the most important skills of harmonious living.

However, not all children are equally good at this. Those whose behaviour is less pro-social tend to be rejected by other children and the pattern of rejection tends to continue. In one study some 15 per cent of 5-year-old children were rejected and two-thirds of these children were still rejected at the age of 8.[183] In another study, children who insisted on their own way at age 4 were much more likely to become bullies and victims of bullying at a later age.[184] While more aggressive themselves, they were prone to attribute aggression to others.

Under the age of 5 most young children are relatively unaware of social class or social differences. But as they get to 7 and older, such issues of identity become more important. Children tend to form groups and behave better to others within the group than they do to outsiders.[185] This tendency to prejudice and tribalism is something which the adult world has to discourage.

It matters in any society, but in a multi-ethnic society like ours it is especially important. The encouraging news is that young people are increasingly free of racial prejudice. When they are asked directly whether they are prejudiced against people of other races only 1 per cent of teenagers say they are 'very prejudiced' and 18 per cent say they are 'a little prejudiced'.[186] This compares with

2 per cent and 26 per cent in the mid-1990s. But any prejudice is too much.

A Moral Vocabulary

Clearly parents have the biggest influence on children's values. But schools also make a major difference. Schools where retaliation is considered normal suffer from more violence and more bullying. Moreover, if society wants to influence parents, one important avenue of approach is through schools. What is needed is a common vocabulary that is used by both teachers and parents.

So how can adults help children to acquire good values? Example is surely better than precept, but both matter. In fact the words we use have a powerful influence on our actions. They work in two ways. They echo in our mind, reminding ourselves of how we would like to be. And they can reverberate in a community, providing a common focus for people's aspirations. So moral education is not fully effective if it is no more than teaching children how to get along with each other. It needs to offer a vision of a good person and a good society.

We can illustrate our point by the practice in schools which describe themselves as 'values-based schools'.[187] Typically the school – its staff, parents and children – agree on a list of words which embody the values of the school. In West Kidlington School in Oxfordshire there are twenty-two values words. These include:

Respect	Trust	Courage	Hope
Caring	Tolerance	Honesty	Love
Responsibility	Understanding	Humility	Peace
Cooperation	Patience	Gratitude	Generosity

Each word acts in turn as the word of the month and gets written prominently on walls around the school. It forms the basis for assemblies and some other lessons, and for discussion between teachers and children when behaviour comes into question.

The question you are asked to consider is: 'What am I like when I am the person I would like to be?' Teachers are expected to practise the same principles as the children. And parents are included at every step. There is strong emphasis on the need for non-violence, both physical and psychological. And there are periods of silent sitting, reflecting on your inner self and how you are contributing to the needs of others. There is good evidence that such silent sitting improves well-being.[188]

Social and Emotional Learning

Values are essentially moral concepts. But how to live up to your values is a matter of psychological capacity. If you are torn apart by anger or greed, it is not easy to live up to good values, even if in principle you subscribe to them. So it is essential that children learn to understand their own emotions and develop strategies for managing their emotions and for cultivating the positive parts of their nature – their better self.

At the same time they can learn in a systematic way how to understand other people – how to avoid attributing malign intent where none is present, how to respond constructively when it is; and in general how to bring out the best in others. All of this contributes to what may be called emotional intelligence.[189] These are 'life skills' that can be taught. For example, Martin Seligman, the father of positive psychology, has developed a Resilience Programme for 11-year-olds which teaches children how to manage their own feelings, and how to understand others and care for them. It takes altogether eighteen hours, with children in groups of fifteen. The results have now been evaluated in twelve random-controlled trials, and the average effect is to reduce the number who suffer depression in the following three years by a half, and the number who behave badly by a third.[190]

These are worthwhile results. In the USA there are hundreds of programmes that aim to improve emotional balance and reduce bad or dangerous behaviour. In an analysis of 200 such controlled experiments the average effect was to raise emotional well-being by over 10 percentile points over the range 1–100 (the most successful programmes of course did more than this). Effects on behaviour were similar in size, and so too was the effect on academic performance.[191]

These findings are of great importance because they show there is no conflict between helping children manage their emotions and improving their school work. A person who can regulate her emotions is usually someone who can also regulate her work effort. Both are important and they are not generally inconsistent with each other. Happy children make better students.

All of this research provides a powerful argument for the teaching of social and emotional learning as a subject in schools. The school itself should embody the values being taught and the teachers should live them out throughout the week.[192] But there should also be at least one time in the week when children specifically develop these skills.

In Britain, this happens through the teaching of Personal, Social and Health Education – or, to use more normal English, life skills. In primary schools the teaching of this is much better performed than in secondary schools, where big changes are needed. The subject mostly gets an hour a week,[193] but this time could be much better used – with better content and better-trained teachers.

The range of topics which needs to be covered is really demanding:

- understanding and managing your emotions
- understanding and caring for others
- love, sex, parenting and child development
- healthy living: exercise, diet, alcohol, drugs, smoking
- mental illness
- your career and contribution to the world
- understanding the media
- politics and responsibilities to the planet
- moral philosophy

These are difficult subjects to teach but together they form a coherent field, based mainly on psychology. Like other difficult subjects, they cannot be taught effectively except by people who have been seriously trained to teach them. It follows that in secondary schools this should be a specialist subject for which a graduate could train in their Postgraduate Certificate of Education. If this happened, it would bring into schools a new cohort, as it were, of missionaries for harmonious living. They would of course need the full support of the head, but they could in turn help the head in improving the ethos of the school as a friendly and non-violent community.

Much of this vision is already implicit in the government's policy. A programme called Social and Emotional Aspects of Learning (SEAL) is now used in most primary schools and is being rolled out in secondary schools, year by year, beginning with 11-year-olds in 2007. The programme focuses heavily on changing the overall school ethos and improving teachers' sensitivity to emotional issues. But it also provides dedicated teaching materials which can be used as part of the teaching of PSHE. As time goes on, the programme should increasingly rely on evidence-based materials, whose impact on children has been thoroughly evaluated.[194] And, for serious results, we need that cohort of dedicated teachers, committed to better relationships throughout the school.

Social Capital

Schools cannot do the job unaided, however. Parents are even more important, but so is society as a whole – what has been called our social capital. We experience others not just in the family, the school and the workplace but in the whole network of social institutions to which we belong – the faith group, the club, the music society, the Red Cross, the group that takes old people on outings. These are institutions that support us in the values we hold, and through which we can express our generous and positive impulses. For religious communities this is an explicit aim.

Throughout history old networks have broken down and new ones developed. In the United States there has been a clear decline in involvement in such groups but no clear decline in Britain – up to 1991 at least when the last count was taken.[195] But for a values-based society it is essential that we sustain these links.

Uplifting Experience

If good human relationships are central to our values, they are not the end of the story. Human beings have always sought something more than that – a spiritual dimension which lights up their inner life. This remains true even in an anti-heroic age when grand perspectives have become suspect. People have an instinct for wonder, and two sources of wonder have always elevated the human spirit.

One is the feeling of belonging to something bigger than oneself – something that gives meaning to one's own small existence.[196] Religious people experience this. Or it can come from music, dance, drama, painting – from anything that takes you out of yourself, and makes you thankful for what you have rather than focusing on what you have not. It comes from involvement in something greater than yourself.

A second key element in the inner life is the astonishing fact that in the end no one can determine your inner state except you yourself. Victor Frankl said of his experience in Auschwitz that 'everything can be taken from a man but one thing, the last of human freedoms – to choose one's attitude in any given set of circumstances.'[197] An essential element in a good life is the feeling that you are the captain of your soul, and that in the end things can be all right inside you whatever happens outside. If you have your own inner life, it becomes more possible to treat the misfortunes of life as opportunities to rise to a challenge.

Both of these almost mystical feelings are crucial for the good life: the feeling of smallness within a greater whole, and the feeling that in the end your inner self is safe. These feelings complement each other, since you cannot feel safe if you are obsessed about yourself and unconnected to something bigger. Our culture does not contain enough of either feeling, since excessive individualism and excessive competition are inimical to both.

RECOMMENDATIONS

We are arguing for a significant change of heart in our society, where adults (be they parents or teachers) are less embarrassed to stand for the values without which a society cannot flourish. This does not mean being more bossy towards children. On the contrary, it means living the values yourself and being confident enough about what is right, so that you can listen to children and discuss with them openly the principles of behaviour and the inner life. In particular we want to emphasize four points.

Moral vocabulary

Parents and teachers should respond positively to children's interest in values. They should exemplify and teach children the importance of key values (like respect, honesty, kindness), using the power of words in addition to example. The power of words should not be underestimated and can be illustrated through the lives of outstanding role-models (who compare well with many existing celebrities).

Social and emotional learning in schools

Every school, whether a faith or a community school, should be in its own way a values school.[198] The school ethos should be built on principles of respect, participation and non-violence, physical and psychological. And there should be systematic development of self-understanding and pro-social behaviour in children (especially through Personal, Social and Health Education). Social and emotional learning should be treated in all courses of teacher training. All schools should have major involvement in the community, and volunteering should become a standard experience available to every child.[199]

Personal, Social and Health Education (PSHE)

PSHE in secondary schools should be taught by specialist teachers, and should become a specialist option in the Postgraduate Certificate of Education. Teachers should, where possible, use evidence-based materials.

Spiritual development

Children should be helped to develop the spiritual qualities of wonder and inner peace – and the sense of something greater than themselves. For different children, religious practice, music, dancing, drama, art, literature, science and the love of nature can all contribute to this experience – as can the understanding of any profound truth. No child is complete without some passionate spiritual engagement of this kind.

The values that children absorb are largely the values of the world around them. Parents start the process and schools continue it. But schools also play other vital roles in the lives of our children.

6. Schooling

I like my school because it has some really cool teachers who make the lessons interesting and really make you want to work.
(13-year-old boy)

Only come to our school if you don't mind not learning in certain subjects as some teachers can't control the class.
(child, age not known)

As W. B. Yeats once said, 'Education is not the filling of a bucket, but the lighting of a fire.' Schools should be transformational – they should expand the powers of the mind, and they should enrich the spirit. Both these roles are vital.

In mental development, the main aim is to produce a love of learning that lasts throughout life, and an ability to learn. Provided this happens, children will learn the subject-matter which they need. If it does not, routine preparation for exams may produce passable results, but it will not produce an educated person. It matters greatly what children learn, but it matters even more that they get the habit and skill of learning.

The development of what used to be called character is also crucial. Here again the key issue is the habits which a child develops – care for others and a capacity for positive living and inner peace. These values come not from being lectured at, but from good role-models who encourage the desire to be a decent person.

So how are schools doing in bringing up educated and decent young people? They are mostly doing well, thanks to the huge dedication of most teachers. Two-thirds of 10-year-olds say that most of the time they like going to school.[200] That is a good start. But there are three areas of concern on which we shall focus:

- Are standards of learning high enough across all schools?
- Is there too much testing, and are there too many league tables?
- Does the atmosphere in our schools support the values we aspire to?

Educational Inequality

So what about our standards of learning? Our system has some outstanding successes. But it also has too many failures. In other words, it is a largely excellent system which is blighted by unequal outcomes. For our more academically minded children, we provide an education as good as most in the world. However, for less academically minded children, especially those from deprived areas, it is often a story of less effective schools, followed by the weakest system of vocational preparation in Western Europe north of the Alps.[201]

Primary schools

The inequality begins in our primary schools. In overall terms, the 1990s saw huge improvements in literacy and numeracy. You can see this in the top two lines in the figure on page 92, which show the percentage of children who leave primary school with the target level of English and Maths.[202] One reason for the improvement was the introduction of the Literacy and Numeracy Strategies in the late 1990s.[203] These strategies are now being supplemented by highly effective Reading Recovery programmes that help to bring the slower learners up to speed.[204] Similar programmes are being developed for mathematics.

It will be essential to focus extra resources on slow learners in this way if the government's targets are to be achieved. For progress on the target has slowed in recent years, as the graph shows.

The biggest problem is the huge variation between schools. Children in schools from deprived areas perform far worse than the national average. This is not true of all such schools – some do extremely well despite adverse circumstances, often due to an inspiring head teacher and highly dedicated teaching staff. But the overall picture is one of huge educational inequalities, closely related to social deprivation.

A goodish measure of whether children are deprived is whether they are on free school meals. So in the table on page 93 we divide schools according to the proportion of their children who are on free school meals. The top

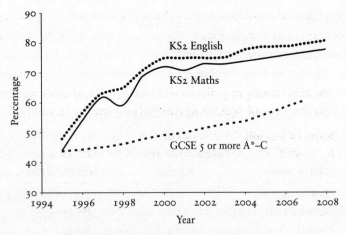

Percentage achieving target at age 10–11 (Key Stage 2) and at age 16 (GCSE)[202]

row of the table opposite relates to the top quarter of schools on that count – that is, to schools with the most deprived children. As can be seen, only 69 per cent of children in these schools achieve their Key Stage 2 target in English. This compares with 89 per cent in the least disadvantaged quarter of schools.[205] The same gap is there in Maths.

Why these differences? In part, it is because the children come to school with greater personal disadvantages. And in part it is because the teaching job is more challenging in these schools.

Teachers find that children in these schools are more difficult to teach and that they spend more time messing around in class. The result is that fewer teachers want to teach in these schools. Though deprived areas attract many excellent teachers, the average teacher there is less experienced and less successful at teaching.[206] Not surprisingly, there is higher teacher turnover, which further disadvantages the children.[207]

Achievement in primary schools: by % of children in the school receiving free school meals (2006)[205]		
Rank of schools by % on free school meals	% of children achieving target in English	(% on free school meals)
Highest quarter	69	(37)
Next quarter	77	(16)
Next quarter	84	(7)
Lowest quarter	89	(2)

It is society's responsibility to break out of this vicious circle. If we are serious about tackling disadvantage, we need to have our most experienced and committed teachers in deprived areas. This would clearly be fairer but it would also be more efficient. For the evidence is that good schools make more difference to disadvantaged children than they do to other children – with bigger effects on their performance.[208] Thus if we compare countries, those where educational performance is more evenly distributed across social classes are those which also get better overall levels of performance.[209]

Secondary schools

The picture of unequal outcomes is even starker in our secondary schools than in our primary schools. By 2006, 45 per cent of all our children were getting five or more GCSE passes at Grades A*–C, including English and Maths. But if we break schools down according to the percentage of children with free school meals (as in the next table), only 28 per cent of children in the most deprived quarter of schools reached that level at GCSE, compared with 67 per cent of children in the least deprived quarter of schools – a much bigger gap than we found earlier between primary schools.

Rank of school by % on free school meals	% of children getting 5 A*–C including English and Maths	(% on free school meals)
Highest quarter	28	(33)
Next quarter	36	(15)
Next quarter	47	(8)
Lowest quarter	67	(3)

School's performance in GCSE: by % of children in the school on free school meals (2006)[205]

In fact almost none of the schools in the most deprived quarter of secondary schools reached the national average standard of performance in GCSE. This can be seen in the following figure where each school's position is indicated by a single diamond. The vertical height of the diamond measures the proportion of children in the school who get free school meals. Its horizontal distance to the right measures the percentage of children achieving good GCSEs. The variation in achievement between schools (on the horizontal axis) is far too great. But, even worse, the schools with high proportions of poor children (on the vertical axis) are almost all in the left-hand, poor-performance part of the diagram.

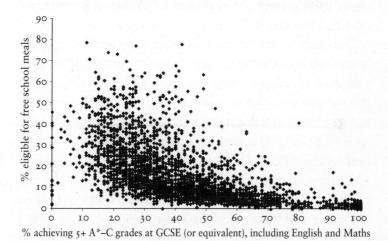

% achieving 5+ A*–C grades at GCSE (or equivalent), including English and Maths

Secondary schools: by level of disadvantage and academic achievement in GCSE[205]

Beyond school

Even so, in terms of average performance British children do not do badly by international standards in their first few years at secondary school. For example, the OECD does a regular survey of the attainments of 15-year-olds in its member countries. In the latest of these 'PISA' surveys our 15-year-olds were ranked in the middle range of countries, together with France and Germany, both in reading and mathematics.[210]

It is when young people move beyond 16 that Britain really drops behind. By their early twenties far more people remain functionally illiterate or innumerate in Britain than in most continental countries north of the Alps. Britain (together with the USA) has a long tail of under-achievers.[211]

This reflects the simple fact that far fewer young people here than in other countries continue with formal education or training beyond the age of 16. The differences can be seen in the following table which looks at the highest level of education a person has reached by the ages of 25–28.[212] The more academic children do as well here as elsewhere – as many complete a higher education (see the first column). But young people who do not complete a higher education do much less well here than in France and Germany. The second column looks at the percentage of our children who reach at least A Level or equivalent (which includes not only higher education but also A Level, Abitur, Baccalaureate, high school graduation and completed apprenticeship). The third column takes a still lower cut-off – equivalent to five good GCSEs. At each level we have fewer people staying on and getting worthwhile qualifications than in France and Germany.

Like the USA we have failed to develop an effective system through which most non-graduates acquire a

	Highest qualification achieved by ages 25–28 (% of cohort)[212]		
	Higher education	At least A Level equivalent	At least good GCSE equivalent
USA	38	58	73
Germany	17	74	85
France	40	62	86
Britain	36	54	73

proper training in a profession, craft or trade. In Germany and France and most other north European countries there are well-developed and well-understood systems of vocational education, including not only on-the-job training but also underpinning theory and continued development of literacy and numeracy, acquired off the job.[213] This is not so in Britain. The effect of this can be seen not only in levels of vocational competence (like our extreme shortage of plumbers) but also in the general educational level of our young adults.

Another tragic reflection of educational failure is the large number of young people aged 16 and over who are doing nothing. They are not still in education or training, but neither has their education been followed by work. As the following table shows, this group, sometimes known as NEETs (not in education, employment or training) has increased in the last ten years[214] – a sad reflection on the effects of their education. The situation is bad for 16 to 18-year-olds but at 19–24 the proportion of NEETs is even higher. A better educational deal for this group of young people has got to be a top national priority.

Percentage not in education, employment or training (NEET) (end of 2006)[214]			
	16	17	18	16–18
1997	6.3	7.8	11.6	8.5
2006	6.5	9.5	14.8	10.3

So what is needed is better schooling for children in deprived areas, and better vocational education for youngsters not going to university. How can it be done?

Teachers

Teachers are the answer to the first of these problems. In a wide-ranging survey of 'How the world's best-performing school systems come out on top', McKinsey's conclude that 'the top performing school systems

(1) consistently attract more able people into the teaching profession
(2) train them well
(3) make sure that every child gets good teaching.'[215]

As illustration, they quote a seminal American study in which students, who started level-pegging at age 8, were by age 11 some 50 percentile points apart (on a scale of 1–100) according to whether they had a high- or low-performing teacher.[216]

This message accords with experience within the English school system. If we look at children in English primary schools, their teachers account for up to 30 per cent of the variance in their progress – a bigger effect than all other aspects of the school put together.[217] So teacher recruitment is the key to educational progress. We urgently need to attract energetic and talented young people into the profession. And we need to ensure that enough good teachers go to where they are most needed – which is in our deprived areas.

Many factors affect who becomes a teacher and where they teach. But there is clear evidence that pay has an effect, especially on men.[218] In the late 1960s the Plowden Report recommended higher pay for teachers in the deprived areas, and this arrangement continued until the late 1980s when it was dropped. There is every reason to re-introduce higher pay for teachers in schools (especially secondary schools) with a high proportion of children on free school meals.

Apprenticeship

After leaving school, young people desperately need good opportunities to learn a skill. The government has taken the bold decision to increase the minimum education leaving age to 18 by 2015.[219] This can be either full- or part-time education. Many young people abhor full-time education, so the new policy can only work if we build a high-quality system of part-time education, linked to apprenticeship where young people can also earn a wage. This is in many ways a more effective system of building real skills than full-time education. It works extremely well in many continental countries, where in Germany, for example, over half the young people complete an apprenticeship. The resulting skill and professional commitment in Germany is there for every traveller to see, and is as evident in hotels and offices as on the factory floor. So apprenticeship is not an old-fashioned approach limited to manufacturing and construction. It is our only hope of ensuring that every youngster has some practicable route to a skill.

This means that every young person with a reasonable school record should be offered an apprenticeship, if that is what they want. The government has accepted this idea and has committed itself to the 'apprenticeship guarantee'. This means that any young person under 18 will by 2015 be guaranteed the offer of an apprenticeship, provided they have five passes at any grade at GCSE and are functionally literate and numerate.[220] These minimum requirements are necessary for employers to be willing to take young people on. For youngsters who do not satisfy the requirements there will be full-time pre-apprenticeship programmes, involving on- and off-the-job experience, to help them qualify.

Serious doubts remain about whether the apprentice guarantee and (with it) universal education and training to 18 will be achieved. Something like a quarter of a million more apprenticeships or jobs with training will

have to be found. To do this by 2015 will be a real
challenge. A National Apprenticeship Service is being
established but it will only be able to do the job if given
enough staff and enough freedom of action. There are
also vital questions over the content of the education
and training. Its purpose is not just to produce specific
on-the-job skills for today's labour market but to provide
underpinning knowledge and general skills like literacy,
numeracy and the ability to interpret and produce docu-
ments. These 'transferable' skills are vital in a changing
labour market and can only be acquired through at least
a day a week (or equivalent) of education or training that
is off the job, rather than at the individual's work station.
It is imperative that this is clearly defined in the framework for all apprenticeships. Though many businesses
have reservations about this, the lawmakers should re-
member that they are building the educational system not
for next year but for the next twenty.

A better deal beyond 16 for less academic young people
is a central plank of any policy for social justice in this
country. At present a young person who goes to university
receives £26,000 of public expenditure on her education
beyond the age of 16;[221] someone who does a full two-
year apprenticeship receives £7,000. That should be an
absolute minimum for all.

Testing and League Tables

Achievement matters at every level, and it is particularly important to support those who struggle most with learning, and thus reduce the social distance which divides group from group. In order to raise standards, governments in the early 1990s introduced standardized tests at 7, 11 and 14 (although in 2008 the government decided to end the tests for 14-year-olds). These tests, together with GCSE at 16, A/S Level at 17, and A Level at 18, make English children the most tested in the world.[222] In addition the government insists that the overall results at 11 and in GCSE and A Level are published for each school, and makes the data for all schools nationally available in a single table, making it easy for the newspapers to construct national league tables of school performance.[223]

Technical problems

There are many problems with these tables. Some come from the design of the tables. First, some published tables give only the raw results, with no adjustment for the type of children going to the school. An alternative indicator is now available which measures children's performance adjusted for their background and their level of attainment before they came to the school. But tables based on these adjusted data get less publicity than the crude, unadjusted ones.

Second, the most publicized scores relate to the percentage of children performing above some cut-off (like the target level of reading or 5 good GCSEs). This score mainly reflects the impact of the school on those children who are near the margin between success and failure. To maximize its score, the school has no reason to improve the scores of children well below the cut-off. This cannot be a healthy situation – where for example it makes no difference what the 30 per cent of children learn who are well below the GCSE cut-off.[224]

To improve the situation, two changes could make a huge difference. First, we should focus on the average performance of all pupils rather than the proportion of them who 'succeed'. And second, we should always standardize each child's performance for their background and, where relevant, their performance when they entered the school.

Effects on motivation and well-being

But there are even bigger issues at stake. Testing and league tables are becoming central to the motivation system of children and teachers, and this raises some fundamental questions.

1. If the main aim of the educational process is to produce exam results, what does this do to a child's *curiosity* and excitement about what she learns? What happens to the child's incentive to explore beyond what will be tested? What happens to the teacher's incentive to inspire? These issues have not been well studied, but

there is a clear danger that education becomes less stimulating when the main incentive is to learn things because they will be tested, and when the fear of failure is a major consideration.[225]

2. How does testing affect the *less academic* children? Certainly it lowers their self-esteem. Before national tests were introduced in England, there was no connection between children's achievement and their self-esteem. But after tests came in, the low-achievers had significantly lower self-esteem.[226] Moreover, testing can hardly fail to influence a school's attitude to low-achievers. Instead of being children in need of help, they can become a threat to the school's reputation – dodgy to admit and a burden to teach.

3. How does testing affect the *quality of life* as children experience it? Here the answer is clear. For many children it casts a cloud.[227] The cloud is both an emotional one and an intellectual one. An over-emphasis on tests lessens the time teachers have to teach topics that do not appear on the test. This narrows the curriculum and stifles pupils' interest. The narrow focus is on 'knowledge and skills', with too little room for teaching related to feelings or social commitment.

In any case, how vital are external testing and league tables for raising educational achievement? Many educational systems depend much less on testing, and do at least as well as England. In Finland for example there is very little external testing, and no inspection, setting or streaming; they invest heavily in teacher training and development, and they come top of the international league in the PISA study of 15-year-olds.[228] Finland also has one of the smallest dispersions in performance. Clearly Finland differs in many respects from England, but (closer to home) Scotland has always had less testing, and Wales and Northern Ireland have now abolished tests, though it is too early to assess the result of this.

Ways forward

So how should our system be modified from the present English system of 'high stakes' tests at 11, 16 and 18? The government is piloting a new system in primary schools where there will be a separate test corresponding to each level of learning.[229] Children will be entered for these 'single-level' tests when their teachers feel they are ready, and they can be entered again if they fail. This approach is part of the government's objective of more personalized learning.

Such regular testing can play a vital role in planning the education of a child, for example by providing the programmes of reading recovery and maths recovery to children who are struggling. But this only requires that the results are known to the child, to parents and the school. If all these new test results were published in a listed form, school by school, it would be totally counter-productive.

For the main use of tests should be to help in the *education of children* and to monitor their progress (i.e. the testing should be 'formative' and internal to the school). Individual children should be the main beneficiaries. This is the direction in which we should move. 'Summative' tests to *evaluate each school*, teacher and pupil should become a less central feature of our system. Education should never be synonymous with teaching to the test.

Values and Discipline

So the first key role of the school is to develop the powers of the mind. But the second key role is equally important – to train the habits of the heart. Most teachers, and most schools, would subscribe to this view.

As we showed in the last chapter, there is no conflict between the objectives of harmonious living and academic excellence. When inner calm is enhanced, better studying results. In fact disruption in the classroom is one of the main impediments to learning.[230]

In many schools today the atmosphere is excellent and highly conducive to learning. But alas this is not true everywhere. In a survey of children aged 11 and 14 in metropolitan areas, 29 per cent said that every day other pupils tried to disrupt their lessons; 43 per cent said that other pupils were 'always' or 'often' so noisy that they found it difficult to work.[231] A nationally representative MORI survey of teachers in 2008[232] again confirmed the frequency of low-level disruption in schools. These teachers reported that in their daily experience:

43 per cent experienced disruption in their lessons

47 per cent experienced answering back

12 per cent experienced abusive or insulting comments

9 per cent experienced damage to property

19 per cent experienced persistent and malicious disruptive behaviour, including open defiance, and

16 per cent experienced a pupil threatening violence to another pupil.

They also reported that at least on a weekly basis:

12 per cent themselves experienced pushing/touching or other unwanted physical contact

9 per cent witnessed violence by a pupil to another member of staff

3 per cent experienced threats of violence to teachers from parents.

The survey showed little change in disruptive behaviour since 2001, but disorder on this scale is highly disturbing. For most teachers the main issue is repeated low-level disruption and impoliteness rather than knives or guns.

What can be done about this? The solution is two-fold. First, schools must act as *values-based communities* promoting mutual respect between all members of the school and involving parents closely.[233] Unless parents are intimately involved in the life of a school, it is not possible to improve the ethos. School councils also have a role to play. Schools need to work really hard with parents, teachers and children to reach agreed standards of behaviour and aspiration. Many schools already do this, and all should.

Second, it is equally important to help individual pupils to manage their emotions. This involves two types of activity. There have to be programmes of social and emotional learning for *all children*, such as we discussed in the last chapter. But there also has to be emotional support for *children in difficulty*, especially those with on-going mental health difficulties such as we discuss in the next chapter.

When a school judges its success with a child, it should look equally at her intellectual progress and her emotional development. Yet schools have batteries of tests to monitor their children's intellectual development – and none to monitor their emotional development. This inevitably risks a distortion towards the goal which is monitored. So we suggest that schools also consider using *standard profiles for emotional well-being* at age 5 (as now) and at 11 (in primary school) and at 14. This would have three purposes: to give the school some measure of its success; to get to know its individual children better; and to help identify those who may need specialist help.[234] The questionnaires would involve parents, teachers and (at 11 and 14) children.[235] This would have to be carefully piloted, including the work which it involved for the school. But it does seem important to provide a counterweight to pressures to neglect this side of the school's work. This is as important in independent schools as it is in the public sector.

RECOMMENDATIONS

So what key improvements are needed?

Teachers' recruitment and pay

It is essential to draw outstanding people into the teaching profession. The greatest need is in schools in deprived areas, which currently have higher teacher turnover and lower average teacher quality than elsewhere. It is essential that children in deprived areas are taught by teachers who are at least as good as elsewhere. This requires among other things a sufficiently large salary differential for teaching in schools which have a high proportion of children on free school meals.

Apprenticeship guarantee

To ensure that every child acquires a skill and continues in meaningful education to 18, every young person with functional literacy and numeracy and five GCSEs at any grade should be guaranteed the offer of a high-quality apprenticeship. Each apprenticeship should include at least a day a week of off-the-job education. Those without these qualifications should take a full-time pre-apprenticeship programme in order to qualify. Finding enough good apprenticeship places must be a top priority for government policy, if our national problems of inequality and low skills are to be seriously addressed.

Attainment tests but no league tables

Tests of attainment should mainly be 'formative' tests to provide feedback to the learner and her parents and to help in planning her education. This is very different from the current 'high-stakes' tests at 11, which are used mainly as tests of the school. The government is now piloting a system in primary schools, where the tests at 11 will be replaced by an annual assessment, including a test at the level for which the child is ready (testing by 'stage not age'). We welcome this direction of change. Under such a system, test results should be analysed within the school, not centrally, and local authorities should provide help with benchmarking, value-added measurement and interpretation.

As regards disclosure, individual children's results should be shared with children and families. The school's benchmarked results should be made available through the school's annual report to current and prospective parents and to the inspectorate. But no public authority should publish tables of results in many different schools. The central government should collect and publish only a sample of results of individual children in order to provide national data as a benchmark against which each school and local authority can measure itself. The same principle about the publication of results should apply to GCSE and A Levels.

We cannot be sure how the press will respond to this more piecemeal release of test results school by school. But at least we should stop having government-sponsored league tables.

Assessing emotional development

Schools should care deeply about the emotional development of their children. It would help greatly if there were a standard assessment of emotional development when children were 5 and 11 (in primary schools) and 14 (in secondary schools). This would provide valuable information on how individual children are doing and also how the school as a whole is doing. It would be information which would be considered by inspectors. This proposal would need to be carefully piloted by the Qualifications and Curriculum Authority and would replace the existing assessment at age 5. All teachers should be taught to recognize mental health difficulties and to know how to respond to them.

School discipline and climate

School discipline can only be based on the ethos of the whole school, which should be based on mutual respect. The values of the school have to be created jointly by the teachers, parents and pupils. Parental involvement is crucial, so that teachers, parents and pupils make common cause.

So far we have mainly talked about children in general. In the next two chapters we focus on children in especial need, beginning with mental health difficulties of the kind we have already alluded to.

What do you think all children and young people need for a good life?

Happy

What are the worst things about your life?

People bullying Me and My Mum having Problems

My Mum

7. Mental Health

Make me have a mum and dad that love me and to start my horid sad life AGAIN and not have so much sadness in my life.
(8-year-old girl)

There's shame with depression, paranoid people are classed as mad, and their own family can be ashamed of it.
(young man in Young Offenders' Institution)

Most of our children lead happy lives, but a minority are seriously troubled or disturbed. Mental health difficulties of this kind are one of the greatest barriers to well-being and a good childhood. Yet only a quarter of the children affected are getting any kind of specialist help.[236]

This neglect is extremely unjust, when these children need so much support. It is also short-sighted, since children who display these difficulties in childhood, if not helped, will be highly likely to become troubled and disturbed adults. Many will continue to be mentally ill, and much more likely than other children to become drug or alcohol addicts, teenage parents or criminals.

Ideally we would have prevented these psychological difficulties before they arise, and we have already discussed many measures which would help to do this.[237] But, if children do have psychological difficulties, the time to help them is early on, when their difficulties are less entrenched and when they are most responsive to good treatment. So just how big is the problem? What causes it, and what can be done to reduce it?

How Many Troubled Children?

According to the government's definitive survey, one in ten of all 5 to 16-year-olds have clinically significant mental health difficulties.[238] Many others, of course, face milder difficulties – but 10 per cent have difficulties that are severe enough to cause major distress or impede their development in important ways. Within this 10 per cent, the types of difficulties that children face can vary widely: some are specific to childhood, but many are childhood counterparts of problems all too familiar in adult life. About 4 per cent of children suffer from emotional difficulties – incapacitating anxieties (about going to school, for example, or being apart from their parents), preoccupying worries, and depression – which, as in adulthood, can shade for some young people into suicidal thoughts and acts. About 6 per cent suffer from conduct disorders – uncontrollable and destructive behaviour, troublesome not only for the child but for all of those around him; if it starts early, it is highly likely to persist into adult life.[239] Others show overactivity and inattentiveness (ADHD), placing major constraints on their learning; while severe developmental difficulties such as autism affect almost all aspects of life.

The full breakdown of difficulties in the table is interesting (many children have more than one condition). Overall, boys have higher rates of conduct disorder than girls, but fewer emotional disorders. For both sexes (but especially girls) the rates of disorder rise with age.

Percentage of children with mental disorder (5 to 16-year-olds, 2004)[238]		
Emotional disorders	3.7	
including anxiety disorders		3.3
depression		0.9
Conduct disorders	5.8	
ADHD*	1.5	
Autistic spectrum disorder	0.9	
Eating disorders	0.3	
Any disorder	9.6	

Note: *Attention Deficit Hyperactivity Disorder. The definition used here is more restrictive than in the USA.

We know that some people dislike the idea of 'diagnosing' children who have psychological difficulties in this way: many of these difficulties have social origins, and there is the obvious danger of labelling children. But there is the even greater danger that we ignore these difficulties, when we could be providing direct and effective help. To do that, a first crucial step is to recognize that children are suffering and in what way.

Is the problem getting worse? Not in recent years:

identical surveys done in 1999 and 2004 show no worsening.[240] But in the decades before 1999, things definitely got worse for teenagers, as we saw in the first chapter.[241] So we are not dealing with a disappearing problem.

What Causes Mental Disturbance?

It has many causes and they involve the intricate interaction of genes and experience.[242] Some children have a greater vulnerability to these difficulties, but how they fare is also affected by their experience. Others are not so genetically vulnerable, but have really bad experiences. All that we can do is to influence the pattern of their experience.

If mental health difficulties have increased, it must be because the quality of children's experience has deteriorated. We have already discussed some of the general influences at work. But we can gain further insight by looking at how mental disturbance varies from one child to another, and see which factors are causing this. Simple correlations between the level of disturbance and each possible cause tell us very little, and we have to rely on the relatively few studies which have tried to look at the simultaneous impact of all the main factors. A recent study took the 1999 national survey of children's mental health difficulties and looked at all the main factors on which information was available. It found, as one would expect, that some obvious characteristics of the child increase the likelihood of disorder – like being older, or male, or in poor physical health, or with a low reading score. It also found that poorer children are more likely than others to have mental health difficulties, but this was mainly because of other key factors which are associated with poverty – lack of income did not cause mental health difficulties directly. When all positive factors were looked at simultaneously the key factors which directly affected mental health included living apart from your father (which increased the risk of difficulties by over 40 per cent), family conflict, poor mental health of a parent, living in rented housing and 'more than 2 adverse life events'.[243]

The survey also makes it possible to follow children for a further three years to see whether their mental health improved or worsened. Once again the underlying variables that made people worse were virtually the same list. And specific life events played an important role – including parental separation, parental mental illness, physical illness of the child and broken friendships.[244]

All of this reinforces the importance of the factors on which we have concentrated in the report, especially stable family life and stable friendships. The strength of the family effect is particularly striking. In nearly every survey the proportion of children with behavioural difficulties is at least 50 per cent higher in families with single parents or step-parents than in families where both parents are still together. Many children of course survive family break-up very well but the risk of difficulties is enhanced.

If a young child has mental health difficulties, these

may well persist unless they get effective treatment – especially if the difficulties are connected with troublesome behaviour. While conduct disorder that begins in adolescence is often temporary (disappearing when adult responsibilities arise), children who are seriously disturbed before they are 10 are highly likely to become disordered adults. For example, if we take children with conduct disorder at age 8, and look at their subsequent record in adolescence, 40 per cent of them were repeatedly convicted of crime. Or, looking back, 90 per cent of adolescents convicted of crime had shown conduct disorder in childhood.[245] More generally, we can see from the table opposite just how strongly severe behavioural difficulties at ages 7 to 9 predict subsequent problems like crime, drugs, teenage pregnancy and welfare dependence in adult life.[246]

What Works?

So what can be done about the problem? We have already discussed a wide range of changes which would produce a healthier society and build resilience in our young people. But for those children who still have difficulties we must make sure they are identified. They should not be stigmatized but their difficulties must be recognized. Many are concerned that this will involve labelling some children as 'mental'. This is indeed a hurdle to overcome. We have to make sure that the stigma attached to identification is, as far as possible, eliminated. We also need to

Subsequent outcomes for children with behavioural difficulties at ages 7 to 9[246]

	Children whose childhood conduct was in	
	worst 5%	best 50%
Percentage subsequently		
committing violent offences (at ages 21–25)	35	3
becoming drug dependent (at ages 21–25)	20	5
having an anti-social personality disorder (at ages 21–25)	17	1
attempting suicide (ever)	18	4
becoming a teenage parent	20	4
becoming welfare dependent (at age 25)	33	9

ensure that what is offered to children with mental health difficulties benefits them to a degree that outweighs the negative effects of whatever stigmatization remains.

The system of services

Apart from parents, those in the best position to identify children who have mental health difficulties are teachers and, for children living in socially disadvantaged families, social workers.[247] The GP will be the first port of call for parents, especially when the children have bodily symptoms such as headaches, stomach pains, chronic tiredness, food refusal, and loss of weight for which there is no adequate physical explanation. These professionals need to be able to identify mental health difficulties, but also to provide sensible advice to parents and young people if the problem exists.

For some children it will be enough to refer the family to the parenting support services which are now being developed nationwide, through training provided by the National Academy of Parenting Practitioners. But if the difficulties are serious, children should be referred for a fully professional assessment from Child and Adolescent Mental Health Services (CAMHS), based within the NHS. This assessment is a key first step. At present many children do not get an assessment of this kind, and a top priority is to ensure that this happens. Enough staff must be trained to do it.

From the assessment emerges an action plan. For many children a multi-disciplinary approach will be needed – as well as help with their behaviour or mood, they may need help with schooling, with disability, with physical problems at home, and so on. Educational psychologists, social workers, nurses and others may have key roles to play. But most children should be under the care of a psychiatrist and receive therapy from a fully trained psychological therapist. Treatments offered should be evidence-based and those offered by CAMHS should normally be those recommended by NICE.[248]

Treatments

There are a number of well-developed treatments that have good records of success and are recommended by the National Institute of Health and Clinical Excellence (NICE). But there are many other practices that make little difference and can waste a lot of money. For example, both psychoanalytic psychotherapy and generic counselling are probably more widely used than is justified by the current evidence as provided by the NICE Guidelines.[249]

So improved treatment is not just a question of more financial resources, but also of which treatments are delivered. For example, in the Fort Bragg experiment conducted in the US professionals were allowed nearly all the resources they wanted, but this made virtually no difference to the children. This was because the treatments offered were not based on sound principles. But there do exist evidence-based programmes of treatment which between them work for the majority of children with mental disorders. Typically they raise a child by ten points in the measure of children's symptoms and well-being (on a scale from 1 to 100).[250]

These programmes work by following well-tried approaches that have been carefully described in manuals, so they can easily be replicated. Usually, the basic ideas are drawn either from 'cognitive behaviour therapy'[251] or from interventions (derived from social learning theory) that change family interactions. For emotional difficulties, such as excessive fearfulness or depression, children are seen alone by the therapist. For behavioural difficulties, the therapist normally works with the parent and child together; and an important part of the treatment is a structured parenting programme.[252] But older children are most commonly seen on their own. For treatments to be most effective there are typically eight to ten sessions (of about an hour each if the child is seen alone, or two hours if the parent is seen as well). And the child's progress is monitored session by session.

It is essential that the therapist is well trained. In one study of a parenting programme for child anti-social behaviour, therapists were independently rated for their level of skill. This was then compared with the results they achieved. The top third of therapists lifted the anti-social children by some 28 percentile points. The least effective therapists actually had a negative effect, as the next figure shows.[253] But even with the most competent therapists, there will be some children whose difficulties are so intractable they will need on-going treatment and care for months or years.

The children who benefit most from these treatments are those with the biggest difficulties (except when these

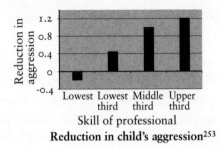

Reduction in child's aggression[253]

are overwhelming). This is a fact of key importance, which is illustrated in the figure below. The light bar shows the level of anti-social behaviour before treatment and the dark bar shows the level after treatment. Those who gain most are those who started with the biggest difficulties. So we get the greatest benefit if we target those who most need treatment. This shows the importance of a really professional assessment.

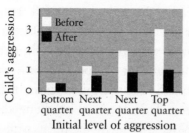

Child's aggression: before and after treatment (according to initial level of aggression)[253]

Better Services

At present only a quarter of children with mental health difficulties get any specialist help. So how can things be improved?[254]

There needs to be a major expansion in CAMHS activity (broadly defined) at all levels: preventive and early identification; parent training; and specialist help for children in difficulty. More resources are needed and improved quality of service. As we have said, teachers must be taught to identify mental health difficulties and respond appropriately. GPs in training should automatically spend at least three months in a community mental health placement. Then parent training needs to be provided on a much wider scale and more professionally: the government already plans to train 6,000 parenting practitioners to work in Children's Centres and other settings.

When it comes to the most specialist services, the key need is for more psychological therapists trained to provide evidence-based therapies. For most of the difficulties which children experience, there is guidance from NICE about which treatments should be provided.[255] These are meant to be the only treatments provided by CAMHS but the guidance is by no means universally followed. This needs to be changed.

In addition there will have to be a well-organized expansion in the total number of therapists. At present they are in such short supply that only the most serious cases can be seen at all. Altogether there are 2,250 clinical psychologists and other therapists in CAMHS.[256] The number has grown rapidly and this growth needs to continue.

To ensure maximum effectiveness we need a five-year plan for child psychological therapy, analogous to the plan for Improved Access to Psychological Therapy which is now being rolled out for adults.[257] This would have two key features: a plan to train or retrain at least 1,000 child psychological therapists in the skills of evidence-based assessment and therapy, and a plan for progressively establishing NICE-recommended services throughout the country.[258] These two features need to be interwoven together, so that the newly trained therapists become properly integrated into the service and the services themselves come closer to implementing the NICE Guidelines. An integrated plan like this has more chance of success, since the training programme gives the Strategic Health Authority for each region the duty of arranging a suitable environment where trainees can get their on-the-job supervised experience. In this way it would be possible to achieve a controlled improvement of both quantity and quality of expert support for children in difficulty. By beginning with a limited number of services, lessons could be learned which could then be applied more widely.

The Costs of Mental Disturbance

The prime reason to act is to relieve the suffering of the children – both now and in their later life. But it costs money.[259] Can we afford it? The answer is Yes, both because it is important and because not doing it currently costs us a great deal. For example, one study followed a sample of 10-year-olds in a South London borough, focusing on those with behavioural difficulties. Their mental health was first measured at the age of 10. Some 3 per cent had conduct disorder – severe and persistent anti-social behaviour – and another 9 per cent had behavioural difficulties, that is, less extreme, but still serious anti-social behaviour. They were then tracked over the next seventeen years until they were 27, and all instances were recorded when they:

- were involved in crime or imprisoned
- went into foster care or children's homes
- received remedial help at school or were excluded.

The table shows the total cost of these experiences to the taxpayer. As can be seen, the children with conduct disorder cost £63,000 more than those without difficulties (mainly due to their greater criminal behaviour). Even if we adjust the figures for all the other characteristics of the child, the 'cost' of the conduct disorder was still £31,000.[260] So this is a problem well worth tackling early, when it is easier to handle. It becomes much more difficult in adolescence.[261]

Costs to the taxpayer of crime, social care and remedial help (from ages 10–27)[260]	
Children with conduct disorder	£70,000
Children with conduct difficulties	£24,000
Children with none of the above	£7,000

In fact good treatments are likely to pay for themselves. For example, in well-designed experiments in the US young offenders have been given functional family therapy or aggression replacement therapy. In each case competent therapy led to major reductions in recidivism which saved the taxpayer $10 for every $1 spent on the therapy. Even when the negative results of poor therapists are included, the taxpayers saved $2 to $7 for each $1 spent.[262]

RECOMMENDATIONS

This chapter has focused on mental disturbance, which affects one in ten children and is also one of our biggest social problems since it contributes to so many other of our problems, such as crime, drugs, teenage pregnancy and educational underperformance. To reduce the amount of mental disturbance among children requires preventive action on many fronts:

- better parenting and family stability   (Chapter 2)
- better lifestyle   (Chapter 4)
- resilience and other training   (Chapter 5)
- reduced educational failure   (Chapter 6)

These are universal approaches. But, for those who suffer despite all this, we need the very best care possible. Mental illness among children should be treated as seriously as any physical illness, and it is not. So what is needed?

Child and Adolescent Mental Health Services (CAMHS)

There should be a major improvement of therapeutic support for parents and their children. This means not just more services but also services that are evidence-based.

Teachers and GPs should be much better trained to identify and support children who are mentally disturbed. Parent training should be available free in Children's Centres and other locations throughout the country. And specialist psychological services need to be radically improved over a five-year planning period. Treatments should be evidence-based, as specified in NICE Guidelines, and some 1,000 professional child therapists need to be trained in the skills of evidence-based assessment and therapy, and integrated within the service. As this training programme proceeds, more and more services, and ultimately all, should be providing, wherever possible, NICE-recommended therapies to all who need them.

Mental disturbance is a major form of deprivation. But so too is material poverty.

8. Inequalities

It is not fair that some people is rich and some are poor.
No one help me and my family.
(10-year-old girl)

To be able to do things without money being a problem because this
country is so expensive especially when you have a big family.
(child, age not known)

After the USA, Britain is the most unequal of the rich countries, and this impacts directly on our children. It is clearest of all when it comes to the distribution of income. Britain has an exceptionally high proportion of children living way below the average standard of living.

In European countries a person is defined as poor if they have below 60 per cent of the typical (median) level of income.[263] This is, as it should be, a relative concept – it shows just how far you are from enjoying the things which other people's children take for granted. In Britain 22 per cent of our children are living in this type of poverty.

That is far from inevitable. As the table shows, the comparable figure in Sweden is only 8 per cent and in Denmark only 10 per cent.[264] Thirty years ago in

**What could be changed
to make life better for all
children and young people?**

makeing everyone
ecwool.

**What could be changed
to make life better for all
children and young people?**

One thing that could be changed is
that not just some people but everyone
had a fave chance at having a good
life.

Britain it was only 13 per cent. So, unfortunately, today's Britain is not the place and time to be at the bottom of the pile.

Percentage of children living in relative poverty, 2005[264]	
Sweden	8
Denmark	10
France	14
Germany	14
UK	22
USA	28
(UK 1979)	(13)

What Poverty Means

To get a feel for what poverty means, one can look at the following table. As it shows, the bottom fifth of children lead radically different lives from the top fifth: fewer or no holidays away, much more cramped living space, fewer places to play or opportunities to swim, and a lack of means to entertain their friends.[265] For parents it means constant embarrassment when children ask: 'Why can't I have what my friend has?'

In an in-depth study of what poverty means, Tess Ridge talked to forty children from low-income families. What the children said to her showed that:

The experience of poverty[265]	Family income per head		
Percentage of children wanting but not having	Bottom fifth	Middle fifth	Top fifth
at least a week's holiday away from home	55	23	3
separate bedrooms for boys and girls over 12	26	13	2
safe outdoor play space	25	12	5
swimming at least once a month	22	6	1
friends round for tea/snacks once a fortnight	17	5	1

- they tried to protect their parents from their own feelings of disadvantage, including sometimes their hunger;
- they felt shame and embarrassment when they were unable to dress like their peers;
- their lives were restricted because of the cost of public transport, and
- they experienced school as exclusionary, often felt unable to go on outings, and felt identified as 'free dinner' children.

This picture of the harsh realities of life with low income was illustrated to us by the Children's Commissioner for Northern Ireland who told us what she meant by poverty. It meant a family who for weeks at a time had human waste coming up through the plughole of the bath. It meant a 15-year-old girl who lied to her parents that she did not want to follow a GCSE Art course, because she knew they would not be able to afford the materials she needed.

Differences between children on this scale are simply unjust. They call for a more equal distribution of income, without the need for further argument.

Inequality and Well-being

There are, however, other arguments as well. For, not surprisingly, poverty is related to many of the other elements of child well-being that we have looked at in this book. Children from poor families fare less well than others in terms of mental health, school achievement, substance abuse and teenage pregnancy. And in terms of later life, poverty in childhood is one of the five most powerful and consistent predictors of subsequent disadvantage.[266]

Similarly, if we compare countries, those with high levels of child poverty also have much worse outcomes for children. This comes out clearly from the UNICEF study, which compared Britain with other countries.[267] For each country we have the level of poverty. We also have an overall index of 'child well-being', calculated to include all factors other than child poverty. We can then ask: How far does the level of 'child well-being' in a country reflect its level of child poverty? The answer is very closely, as the graph below shows.[268] The USA has the most child poverty (measured on the horizontal axis), and it has one of the lowest levels of child well-being (measured on the vertical axis). Norway has the least child poverty, and it has one of the highest levels of child well-being.

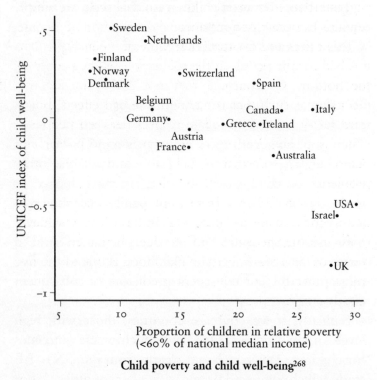

Child poverty and child well-being[268]

So poverty is related to poor outcomes for children. But does this mean that poverty is a direct cause of these outcomes? Only partly. In all studies of individuals, the effect of family income on outcomes is greatly reduced, and even sometimes disappears, when other causes of child well-being are taken into account.[269] Similarly, when we compare Britain with other countries, do our children do worse because so many of them are poor or, alternatively, do our richer children also do worse than equally rich children in other countries? Preliminary evidence suggests that it is mainly the second alternative which explains our poor performance.[270]

This offers an important new view of inequality – that it is bad for the people at the top as well as the people at the bottom. Of course it may not mainly be income inequality as such that is having these bad effects, but a third factor – like inadequate respect between people – which is causing both income inequality and poor child outcomes. That is what we believe is at the root of our problem.

A society which practises less mutual respect will produce many types of bad outcome, and it will also produce more income inequality. To produce better child outcomes we have to change the fundamental ethos and this will produce better child outcomes of all kinds. We must reduce income inequality, but it is not enough. We must also change the overall ethos of our society, making it less success-oriented and more generous with respect. What we are talking about once again is the law of love.

In fact unless we change the overall ethos, it is most unlikely that British governments will persist with poverty reduction. For, though most people now pay lip service to the idea of eliminating child poverty, many have private reservations about whether we should or really could do much to reduce income inequality in this way. We do not agree with them but we must discuss the three main objections which people raise:

- Poverty reduction will reduce incentives and thus reduce average income.
- Social mobility is more important than poverty reduction.
- Poverty reduction is impossible.

Let's look at them one by one.

National Income and Well-Being

Many argue that a society with smaller differentials between rich and poor would indeed have less poverty but this would be at the cost of lower *average* income. On this view the gains from distributing the cake more equally would be more than outweighed by a fall in the total size of the cake. And if we did less to encourage competitive behaviour between people, this would, they argue, do further damage.

We have two comments on this view. First the premise is not necessarily true. If we reduce child poverty, this may not in fact reduce average income. It may empower many more youngsters, so that they become more productive. Moreover, if they behave less competitively at work, and are more cooperative, this too may raise national output.[271]

But, second, suppose the premise is true, and national income is somewhat lower as a result. Is that a disaster?

For example, would it mean that we could no longer compete in the international market place and would therefore lose jobs? Not at all – we should always be able to compete provided our wage levels stayed in line with our productivity. But how would our children fare if national income was lower than it might otherwise be?

To investigate this, we can look again at the differences among the countries which we studied before. How far does the well-being of children appear to depend on the *average* level of income in the country? Among advanced countries, the answer is 'Not at all.' This is illustrated in

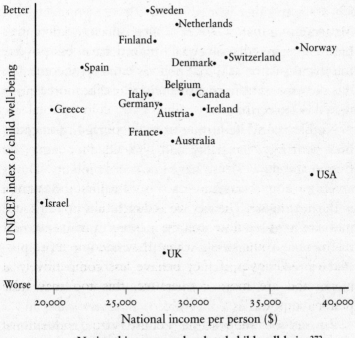

National income per head and child well-being[272]

the figure on page 137.[272] The richest country is the USA and it has one of the lowest levels of child well-being. So average income has little effect on child well-being. But inequality does.

Low Social Mobility

Another common argument is this: It does not matter if children are unequally situated, provided children from poor homes have a good chance of becoming rich, and children from rich homes have a good chance of becoming poor. In other words, it is the level of mobility that matters more than the level of inequality: inequality is all right if everyone has an equal opportunity to be unequal. Indeed it is often said that policies which try to equalize income do so at the cost of social mobility – preventing the poor from rising.

Nothing could be further from the truth. In fact countries with high inequality and high child poverty (like Britain and the US) also have low social mobility. This is a very profound and important truth which is illustrated in the next figure. The way we assess the amount of social mobility is to see how well the parents' income predicts the income of their child when that child is grown up.[273] If the predictive power of parents' income is high, this means that the level of social mobility is low. So this predictive power is a measure of *social immobility*, and it is the one we use. For each country we take men born around 1970 and measure how well their earnings as adults are predicted by their parents' income.[274] We plot this measure of immobility on the vertical axis. As the figure shows, Britain is much more immobile than the Scandinavian countries, and the US is even more immobile. For both Britain and the US their image as especial lands of opportunity is simply a fallacy.

Turning to the horizontal axis, we plot countries according to their level of *child poverty* around 1982 when the men in the sample were around 12 years of age.[275] The results are as we said – the countries with the most child poverty have the greatest levels of immobility. If children start off further apart, it is not surprising that they find it more difficult to change places later on.

So social mobility in Britain is low. Is it getting worse? On some measures, yes. If we stick to income mobility

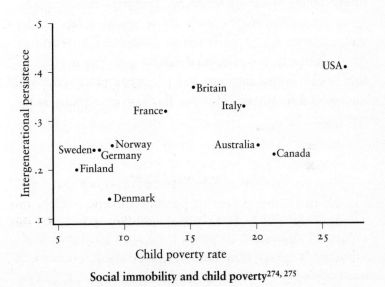

Social immobility and child poverty[274, 275]

as our measure, it has become easier to predict a child's income from her parents' income than it was.[276] This emerges from a study which measured the income of parent and child for two cohorts of children: those born in 1958 and those born in 1970. The child's income was more closely related to the parents' income in the second of these cohorts (who had left school in the 1980s) than in the first (who left school in the 1970s).

Why was this? The main change was a fall in educational opportunity: family income became a better predictor of the educational level achieved by the child. And education is a good predictor of the child's income. Thus, as educational opportunity fell, the family income of the parents became a better predictor of their child's subsequent income.[277] This change in educational opportunity emerges clearly when we compare children who grew up in the 1970s with those growing up in the 1980s. However, since the 1980s, educational opportunity (thus defined) has remained unchanged. So it is likely that social immobility too has in recent years remained unchanged in Britain. But the level of immobility is far too high.[278]

Cutting Child Poverty

Thus we conclude very firmly that child poverty and inequality should be reduced. But can it be done? With immense courage the Labour government committed itself in 1999 to abolishing child poverty by 2020, getting half way there by 2010. But progress has been slow. By 2006/7 the child poverty rate had only been reduced to 22 per cent – from 26 per cent in 1998/9.[279]

We must do better. Child poverty is already much lower in many other countries than it is here and, as the figure below shows, it was much lower here in most of the post-war period.[280] There is now little hope of hitting the 2010 target but there should be an absolute commitment to hitting the figure for 2015 that is implicit in the government's target (which is 6.5 per cent).

To cut child poverty, three main factors are involved. The first is whether the parents work. We still have the largest proportion of households in Europe in which no parent is working. This is a major failure, resulting largely from ill-thought-out welfare policies over many decades. New government initiatives on welfare-to-work should make a substantial difference.[281]

The second factor is how much workers earn. In Britain,

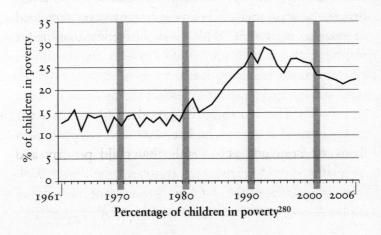

Percentage of children in poverty[280]

earnings became much more unequal in the 1980s, and even with the help of the national minimum wage there has been little reduction in the dispersion of earnings except at the very lowest end. A key reason for this on-going inequality is the unequal schooling we have described and the disastrous failure of our system of training for youngsters not headed toward university. Improvements here could have a large effect in reducing low pay.

But then there is the third factor – the impact of taxes, tax credits and benefits. The present government has made this system substantially more redistributive.[282] But to hit the child poverty target, more redistribution will be needed. At present an unchanged fiscal policy would automatically lead to an annual increase in child poverty, because most benefits and tax credits relevant to children are indexed to prices rather than earnings, or not indexed at all. Since earnings normally rise faster than prices, this means that earnings normally rise faster than benefits and tax credits – driving more of those who depend on benefits and tax credits downwards across the threshold of relative poverty.[283] This is an absurdity that needs stopping; all the relevant benefits and tax credits should be indexed to earnings. But on top of this, substantial sums will have to be spent in further raising these benefits and credits. This has to be a top priority for any government, even if it means higher taxes and redistribution from childless families to those with children.

Looked-after Children

However, material deprivation is not the only kind of deprivation, nor the only form of inequality. Another is mental disturbance, which we have already discussed. And there are many other groups of deprived children as well – including those with physical disabilities, those with learning difficulties, children from ethnic minorities and children who are refugees. But, as we explained in Chapter 1, we cannot do justice to the needs of all these groups – and many have been well covered in other reports.[284] But there are two groups that we must consider because we as a society are directly responsible for them, and because they desperately need better care.

The first are children who are 'looked-after' by local authorities, because they do not have parents and family who can look after them properly. At any given time there are 60,000 like this in England and Wales – just over 1 in 200 of our children. They stay in care for about two and a half years on average and then return to their families or cross the threshold into adulthood. While in care, the majority are in foster families but some are in residential homes. Over 60 per cent of these children came into care because of abuse or neglect. Most of the rest are there because of family dysfunction or disaster, or because of absent parents – including 3,000 unaccompanied refugee children.

Many of these children are severely deprived. Half suffer from mental health difficulties,[285] and a disproportionate number are from ethnic minority backgrounds or are physically disabled. The evidence on the life chances for these children makes depressing reading. They are much less likely than average to get good GCSEs or to move on to further or higher education. And they are much more likely than average to become teenage parents, to spend time in custody, and to have drug problems. Former cared-for children comprise 27 per cent of the prison population.[286]

Of course, these negative 'outcomes' cannot be seen as simply the result of being 'looked after'. As we have seen, most of these children only spend a small part of their childhood in care, and most are already disadvantaged before being 'looked after'. However, in intervening in these children's lives the state has an opportunity, and a responsibility, to improve their well-being. As the Nottingham City Council put it:

Some may say that part of the reason . . . [for poor outcomes] . . . is that children who enter care come disproportionately from poor backgrounds and have complex needs, but it is inexcusable and shameful that the care system seems all too often to reinforce this early disadvantage, rather than helping children to successfully overcome it.[287]

The worst thing is the lack in continuity of care: the average placement in a foster family or home is eight months, meaning four placements on average. In most of the homes the turnover rate of staff is also very high, and high turnover of social workers presents a further stumbling-block to continuity of care. How can a child learn to live and love in such a circumstance? Not easy. It is not surprising that the more stable the placement the better the subsequent outcome (on average) for the child.[288]

We must ensure a better standard of care. The first step is better training and better financial rewards for those who do the caring. Another is better organization in social services departments. And a third is to ensure that every child gets a fully professional mental health assessment as soon as they are taken into care.[289] Finally, how can it be right for the state as parent to cease its responsibilities when a person reaches 18 when a half of all other young people aged 20–24 are still living at home?[290]

Children in Custody

A closely related group of young people are those taken into custody – nearly half of whom were previously in care.[291] We currently have 3,000 young people under 18 in custody. They stay inside on average for four and a half months, so roughly 8,000 go into custody each year.

Most of these young people are severely deprived.[292] Nearly half have literacy and numeracy levels below the norm for 11-year-olds. Of the girls, 40 per cent have suffered violence at home, often sexual abuse, and so have 25 per cent of the boys. Two-thirds are from broken homes. At least a third have serious mental health needs, yet very few have even received an assessment, let alone treatment.[293]

These are young people in need. Of course society has to protect itself, but we shall never develop effective protection unless we also recognize the needs of the young offenders. Custody should be the last resort. Our rate of incarceration of young people is one of the highest in Europe and our age of criminal responsibility (at 10) is one of the lowest.

Our best protection is to help these young people earlier.[294] Their needs are the same as for children in care: better support, from the same professionals, for years on end[295] – and an early assessment so that the right strategy can be put in place. Even if they end up in custody (with all the boundaries that implies) they should be cared for as much as any other child.[296]

Overlapping Inequalities

Some groups of children are more likely than average to experience poverty. These include children in minority ethnic groups, disabled children, children living with a disabled parent, Traveller and Gypsy children, children living in lone-parent households, and children living in large families. A recent review for the Joseph Rowntree Foundation highlighted the substantial differences in child poverty across different ethnic communities, with particularly high rates for children of Pakistani, Bangladeshi and Black African origins.[297] Destitution (extreme poverty, creating homelessness and persistent hunger) among asylum-seeking and refugee families has a highly negative impact on the lives of children in these families.[298]

The different types of inequality we have discussed do not exist in isolation. Many are connected to each other and many children experience more than one of these inequalities for some or all of their childhood.

Combinations of inequalities can have a drastic effect on children's life chances. Research has shown that a young person aged 13 or 14 experiencing five or more problems in the family environment – such as mental health problems, physical disability, substance misuse, domestic violence, financial stress, neither parent being in work, teenage parenthood, poor basic skills and living in poor housing conditions – is thirty-six times as likely to be excluded from school and six times as likely to enter the care system or have contact with the police as a young person living in a family with none of these problems.[299]

Discrimination

Some inequalities in wealth or other outcomes are the result of identifiable discrimination against certain people and groups, some are not. Discrimination is damaging in itself. The experience of being treated unfairly or disregarded because of who you are, exposure to negative and belittling attitudes, or being a victim of bullying, aggression or harassment born out of prejudice, are also damaging.

A study of individuals aged 15 and over in England

undertaken by MORI in 2001 suggested that almost two-thirds were prejudiced against at least one minority group.[300] The most common groups that people said they were prejudiced against were refugees/asylum seekers and travellers/gypsies (around 14 per cent of respondents mentioned each group) with people from minority ethnic groups and gay and lesbian people being the next most common groups (around 7 per cent each). Clearly these prejudicial attitudes are likely to affect children and young people in these groups as well as adults.

In the same way as economic inequality damages our whole society, discriminatory attitudes and behaviours are not only acutely damaging for the individuals they target, but for all children who grow up witnessing and absorbing such disrespect as a part of our social fabric. We must acknowledge that prejudice and discrimination are significant barriers to creating the kind of caring, respectful society in which all children can flourish.

RECOMMENDATIONS

This brings us to our three final recommendations.

Cutting child poverty

The government should make much more serious efforts to achieve its target of poverty reduction. This would mean cutting the child poverty rate to 6.5 per cent by 2015. One vital step is to index benefits and tax credits to earnings, but this will only hold the present situation. Further major commitments are needed if poverty is to be further reduced.[301]

Continuity of care

Children 'looked-after' by the state and those in custody should have much better care. The central principle should be that they are cared for by the same carers (or workers in children's homes) for as long as possible. This principle should never be sacrificed to administrative tidiness. A second principle is that all children coming into care or into custody should have a fully professional mental health assessment and, where appropriate, treatment. A final principle is that custody should be absolutely the last resort.

Pay and status

None of our objectives in this book can be achieved unless working with children becomes a more highly esteemed vocation. Social care of children requires more training and better pay than it currently receives. This means that the services themselves need to be better resourced. Our children deserve no less, and society as a whole will reap the reward.

In parallel with this, we have to create a society in which there is a more egalitarian and caring ethos. In fact no government will incur the massive costs needed to eliminate child poverty unless there is a major change in public values. That is why values provide the overarching theme of this report.

9. Conclusions

I think the things that stop children and young people from having a good life are: wars, unkind people, parents that argue and split up, not having parents, not having enough food and water and not being able to live feeling safe.

(9-year-old girl)

We can make a better world for our children. Three words best sum up our message.

The first is *love*. That is what children say they want, more than anything else. And, if well cared for, that is what they learn to give. For this to happen, they need parents and teachers who are unselfish and from whom they learn the secret of harmonious living: putting human relationships above all else. We want our children to discover that caring for others and contributing to a common good is ultimately more satisfying than either wealth, beauty or personal success. This will require a radical shift away from the excessively individualistic ethos which now prevails, to an ethos where the constant question is 'What would we do if our aim was a world based on love?'

The second word is *respect* – respect of adults for children, and of children for others. We cannot help our

What are the best things about your life?

having my mom for a friend

What do you think all children and young people need for a good life?

A good family ♪

children unless we respect them as infinitely precious people, whose feelings and thoughts are of the greatest importance. Children are not 'incomplete adults'; their current quality of life is as important as the future adults they will become. They need listening to.

In today's world respect has to be mutual, not hierarchical. Automatic deference to rulers, teachers and parents is a thing of the past. For some parents this is a problem, but the answer is not permissive parenting where anything goes. Children need unconditional love of them as persons, but they also need clear boundaries, based on reasoned explanation. All the evidence shows that this pattern of 'authoritative' parenting is the best.

Parents must of course live the principles they purport to believe in. Interestingly, the countries which rate highest for child well-being (Denmark, Sweden and the Netherlands) are those where adults are most inclined to agree that 'one does not have the duty to respect and love parents who have not earned it by their behaviour and attitudes'.[302]

If parents respect their children, their children will with luck respect others. A harmonious world can only be based on the principle that each human being matters equally. This includes children. We need a society which values children more highly. Proposals to put curfews on children or to expose them to ultra-sonic deterrents or to ban them from parts of town are out of order and an offence against their rights. So is huge economic inequality.

The third word is *evidence*. Many of the topics in

this book are highly emotive. We shall not solve them except on the basis of evidence and its interpretation. That has been our approach and we give the evidence in the various chapters of the book – we do not report it here.

Until recently, people thought that the inner subjective quality of life was beyond the scope of scientific inquiry. Partly for this reason, excessive interest focused on the externals of a person's life – above all their wealth and success. But today psychologists can assess the inner states of children, as well as their behaviour. As a result we have learned a lot about what works to improve the experience of childhood, and what does not; and this has enabled us to place the mental health and well-being of children much nearer the centre of our thinking.

This ought to be a time of hope for children in Britain. There is more discussion than ever about the lives of our children. The government has produced an imaginative Children's Plan and on many counts the lives of children are improving.[303] But much remains to be done – by parents, teachers, government, media and society at large. In this report we have traversed the lives of children at each stage from birth onwards, and have produced recommendations for each stage – based on evidence and with the reasoning explained. In what follows we re-group the recommendations according to the group of people to whom they are addressed – parents, teachers, government, media, and society at large. For convenience we present the recommendations concisely, and without the reasoning which can be found in the relevant chapters.

So who should do what?

Parents

- The greatest responsibility is on parents. The most important act which two people ever perform is to bring another being into the world. This is an awesome responsibility and, when they have a child, the parents should have a *long-term commitment to each other* as well as to the welfare of the child.
- Before the child is born (especially the first child) the parents should be *fully informed* of what is involved in bringing up the child – the physical and emotional care of the child and the impact on their own relationship. So parenting classes covering these topics should be available to both fathers and mothers around the time of the birth.
- Children need above all to be loved and to have parents who love each other. But good parenting also involves the ability to establish *boundaries* – parenting sometimes called authoritative.
- Parents and teachers should not hesitate to discuss moral principles with their children. A good *moral vocabulary* is a key resource for every child and future adult. Children should learn that a life devoted to something bigger than yourself is ultimately more satisfying than one devoted to more selfish ends.

- And parents should live the principles which they encourage in their children. Above all, *parents should aim to live harmoniously* with each other, which is one of the deepest desires of every child.
- If both parents are going to work, the *transition to full-time childcare by other carers* should be gradual, and parental care should be replaced by high-quality and consistent childcare, provided by well-trained people. Equally, parental leave with job security should be available for longer periods, as in France and Germany.
- Parents and teachers should recognize how important *friends* are to children and not disrupt their friendships except for good reason.
- Children should take *physical exercise* (more than just walking) for at least seven hours a week, and parents and teachers should make this possible.
- Parents and teachers should help their children to develop the *spiritual qualities* of wonder and inner peace – and the feeling of something greater than themselves.

Teachers

- Schools have a key role. They should promote not only academic skills but also help children to develop *happy, likeable and pro-social personalities.* This requires both a good school ethos, and the right approach to individual children.
- In too many schools, the ethos is one of struggle between teachers and children and discipline is poor.

Discipline can only be based on a deeply ingrained pattern of *mutual respect*, shown by teacher to teacher, by teachers to pupils, by pupils to teachers, and by pupil to pupil. This, linked to firmness and interesting teaching, is the foundation for good discipline and an effective learning environment in a school. It can be achieved even in areas of deprivation, and often is. It is essential that children in deprived areas are taught at least as well or even better than elsewhere.

- *Physical and psychological violence* should be out of order in a school and in a home. Every teacher should be taught to identify and deal with bullying. School discipline should be based on values and procedures worked out with and shared with parents and children.

- Social and emotional learning is important not only for psychological well-being but also for good academic performance. It requires not just a good school ethos but also deliberate teaching of social and life skills in dedicated time. This happens quite well in most primary schools, but poorly in many secondary schools. In secondary schools *Personal, Social and Health Education* (PSHE) should be taught by specialist teachers, trained for the purpose in their Postgraduate Certificate of Education.

- PSHE should cover not only understanding yourself and social behaviour, but also sex and relationships, parenting skills, child development, understanding the media, and volunteering. *Sex and relationships education* should be presented not as biology but as a part of social and emotional learning.

- On the personal development of children, there are three problems: to make schools view it as seriously as they view academic progress; to help schools know their children; and to identify children with mental health difficulties. For all these reasons, it would help if schools administered *standard assessments of emotional and behavioural well-being* to all students at 5, 11 (in primary school) and 14. Such a proposal should be carefully piloted. All teachers in training should also be taught about mental health difficulties: how to recognize them and how to respond.

Government

- Government too has its role. For children whose birth is not celebrated through a religious ceremony like christening, there should be a *civil birth ceremony*. This could normally be when the child is between 6 and 12 months old. It would be performed like a civil marriage by the local Registrar with friends and relations present, unless the parents wished to opt out.
- High-quality services should be available throughout the country to *support parents*:
  - parenting classes available free around the time of the birth of the child
  - psychological support if their own relationship is in danger of breaking up or does so
  - parenting support if the child develops behavioural or emotional difficulties

- specialist support through Child and Adolescent Mental Health services if the child is severely disturbed.

These services are so important to children's welfare that they should be available free. Though many of them can be delivered by voluntary agencies, they should be co-ordinated and guaranteed by the NHS.

- Existing *Child and Adolescent Mental Health Services* need radical improvement. They need to be more readily available (more quantity) and more evidence-based (better quality). The greatest need is for more high-quality psychological therapists, and a five-year plan is needed to train at least 1,000 more of them in the skills of assessment and therapy. From society's point of view it would be money well spent and would probably pay for itself.

- *Looked-after children* (in the care of local authorities) and *children in custody* need especial care, and should automatically receive a mental health assessment and treatment if necessary. The turnover of carers in children's homes and children's services should be dramatically reduced.

- All *people who work with children including teachers and childcare workers* are doing work of enormous social value. This should be better reflected in their pay and status.

- To reduce educational inequality, *teachers in deprived areas* should receive a salary supplement sufficient to ensure that teacher quality and levels of turnover in these areas are at least as satisfactory as elsewhere.

- The present system of *tests for academic performance* needs replacing. The 'high-stakes' tests at 11 should be replaced by an annual assessment of each child, designed mainly to guide the child's learning. Present government thinking is on the right lines.
- The government should stop publishing data on individual schools from which *league tables* are constructed. It should only publish the distribution of performance across all children in the country, so that each school can compare its performance with that in other schools.
- Young people with a mainly practical bent should be guaranteed a clear pathway to a skill through the offer of an *apprenticeship*. This needs to become a central aspect of educational policy, and a major campaign should be launched to persuade employers to provide the places.
- There should be a really high-quality *Youth Centre* for every 5,000 young people, with facilities for sports, music, art, dance, drama and volunteering as well as psychological therapy, health guidance and vocational guidance.
- *No sports fields or open spaces where children play* should be built on, without the provision of equivalent open space elsewhere.
- Firms selling goods and services in Britain should be *banned from placing media advertising aimed at British children under 12*. And, to improve adolescent health and behaviour, *alcohol* should be much more highly taxed (while adjusting other taxes to offset any extra burden on poor people). Neither alcohol nor unhealthy food should be advertised on television before 9 p.m.

- By 2015 the proportion of *children in relative poverty* should be reduced from 22 per cent in 2006/7 to under 10 per cent, as in the Scandinavian countries.

The Media

As they grow older, children increasingly absorb their values from the media. They watch television or use computer-based media for an average of four hours a day. The impact of this is well attested in the evidence. So people who put material out on these media should reflect in their hearts on how this material impacts on the welfare of children. They should be embarrassed at the amount of physical violence which they put out, and advertisers should be embarrassed at their encouragement of premature sexualization, heavy drinking, and over-eating.

The media should also re-think the way they present the lives of children. They give a totally unbalanced impression of the risks which children face from strangers, and they encourage a culture where children find it ever more difficult to practise their natural urge to explore. The media also promote an exaggerated picture of young people threatening our social stability.

Society at Large

We need a more positive attitude to children, where we welcome them into our society and want to help them. Constant criticism does no good. We have described a whole series of changes which would improve their lives. But most of all our adult society has to change. For in the end the values which children absorb will be the values of the adult society around them. In recent decades traditional beliefs have weakened and the void has been filled by an excessive individualism, which holds that our main duty is to make the most of ourselves. Too often this means being as successful as possible, in what becomes a struggle of each against all.

In consequence there has been a decline in the sense of fellowship which holds society together. This has eroded the bonds of trust between us, and children suffer as a result. There are, however, countries in which trust has not declined. In Denmark, Sweden and the Netherlands around two-thirds of people believe that most people can be trusted – twice as many as in Britain and the USA.[304] It is no coincidence that these are also the countries where, according to the UNICEF report, child well-being is highest.

So it is possible to construct a modern society in which there are higher levels of child well-being than in Britain. The key is an ethic in which we care more for each other. As the psychological evidence shows, this yields a double benefit – other people treat us better and we feel better from helping them. It is a world like this, built on the law of love, that we should create with our children.

Messages for Young People

During panel meetings groups of children and young people came to present their own experiences to the panel. These meetings were significant in helping the inquiry to be grounded in children's own experiences and ideas. Although the inquiry report is written for an adult audience there are messages that the panel want to make to children themselves, particularly about issues that children can control.

Family

When parents argue they sometimes forget their children are upset and perhaps don't realize you can be frightened to see them angry with each other. It may be difficult to do, but tell them how upset you are made by their quarrelling. If you stay upset, try and find someone you can talk to – a friend, teacher, youth worker, someone you can trust.

Friends

Your friends may well be the best thing in your lives. You are bound to have disagreements with them from time to time. But try to keep your friends even if you disagree with them. Losing friends is really painful. Having friends that last for a lifetime is like finding treasure. So try to sort out problems with friends by listening and talking, not by breaking up.

Lifestyle

It is important that children have lots of opportunities to play outdoors and enjoy organized sports. Look around your neighbourhood for safe and fun places to play. If you think that places are unsafe or too untidy to play in then get in contact yourself with your local council and ask them to make the place safer or tidy it up, or ask your parents to contact them.

Getting drunk is not a clever thing for adults to do, let alone children. They risk getting into trouble, letting themselves down and making themselves feel ill. We don't want children and young people to follow adult behaviour and drink too much. You should resist pressure to do so and encourage your friends to do the same.

Having sex is a choice when the time is right, not something you have to do. One bad reason for having sex is that you get pressured into it, or think that everyone else is doing it so you have to as well. You don't have to give in to these pressures and it is better that sex is with someone you have known for a long time and really love, not just find attractive. In many religious and cultural traditions sex is not allowed outside of marriage.

Health

Staying fit and eating healthily are important. So make sure you get at least seven hours of proper exercise a week. You know which are the healthy and which the unhealthy foods with loads of fat and sugar in them. Firms that make food that is bad for you spend a vast amount of money on advertising trying to make you eat their stuff. Don't be fooled.

Values

Children and young people have told us the importance of respect, fairness and kindness. You should be bold in demonstrating these values in your relationships with others, both children and young people and adults.

Some adults behave as if children and young people don't matter, or seem to be cross with seeing groups of children and young people in public. That kind of attitude is unfair, but when you are sharing space with adults, on a bus or in the street, make sure you don't give adults reason to be upset or cross with you.

Some adults are frightened of young people, especially if they see groups of young people walking towards them. The world should be a friendlier place, with adults and young people liking and respecting each other.

Learning

Nearly all children think their school could be a better place if only teachers listened to them more. So make sure, if there is a school council, you use it to say what you think about your school. And if you think one or more of your teachers is really good make sure they know you appreciate them. Some children feel embarrassed to enjoy school, but if you like to learn and do well then be proud to do so. If you find school a struggle, don't give up on learning but make the most of the things that interest you.

Afterword by
Dr Rowan Williams,
Archbishop of Canterbury

A few days before the final draft of this report arrived on my desk, there had been an intriguing media flurry over, of all things, a poem in the English curriculum of secondary schools. Carol Ann Duffy's poem about a frustrated, angry and confused teenager leaving the house with a knife in his or her pocket had been the subject of a small number of complaints on the grounds that it somehow colluded with or 'normalized' knife-carrying, at a time when knife crime involving teenagers had risen to a very disturbing level. One education authority had duly banned the poem, and predictable controversy followed.

The debate was intriguing because it seemed to trade on two of the most powerful and least helpful elements in our thinking about children and young people in this society. On the one hand, the child is appallingly vulnerable, mentally as well as physically; the chief need of a child is protection from what will assault and corrupt. On the other hand, the child is potentially menacing; the condition of many or most of our young people at the moment is almost feral, and society needs to be protected from them. Clear messages must be sent about what society will and will not tolerate.

To be concerned about protecting children is entirely

right. The last decade has alerted all of us to some of the ways in which we have betrayed children by not securing them against assault and abuse in various contexts, and no one can be complacent in this area. Likewise, it is right to feel with some urgency that a youth subculture in which extreme reactive violence is normal is a terrible thing and needs to be confronted. But dealing responsibly with these anxieties needs some reality-checking and some scrutiny of the mythology of panic. Perhaps above all, it needs some careful listening to how children and young people themselves experience and think about who they are and where they are. It needs to assume that our young people are – no less than adults – capable of being *intelligent*.

The Good Childhood Inquiry has attempted to work on this assumption, and it has painted a detailed and compelling picture of the intelligence of the young people who have contributed to it. It resolutely refuses to give an apocalyptic analysis of a generation out of control; but what it does is to turn a sharp eye on the society in which children are being raised and ask just how it has become so tone-deaf to the real requirements of children. It challenges us about why words like love, happiness and stability have come to sound either bizarre or dull to so many adults, when in fact they are the necessary iron rations for maturity, sense, empathy and everything else needed for a balanced human existence alongside others.

There has been some understandable mockery of the idea that there should be classes in 'happiness'; but we might well wonder why it is that the suggestion was ever made – why it had come to seem that the concept wasn't obvious. And without a coherent sense of what makes for long-term human well-being, the educating of a new generation is hamstrung from the start. The report doesn't quite say that we are without such a coherent sense, but it notes a whole range of things which strongly suggest that there is a huge amount of ground to make up. In particular, our attention is drawn to the effect of obsessive testing in the educational process and how it works for the interests of some parents and some schools, but not in the interests of the children; to the equally obsessive drive to co-opt children into the market-place by intensive advertising; to our casual attitude in the UK towards preparing young people in their mid-teens for a working environment by solid investment in post-school training. These are social habits that might have been deliberately designed to minimize confidence and a steady sense of well-being. But behind these and other specifics, there lie deeper troubles. We tolerate levels of arbitrary violence in our entertainment that have a debasing effect on every-one's imagination. We shy away from confronting the cost that may be involved in preserving stability in our relationships. Despite serious efforts to change the situ-ation, we remain a gravely unequal society, with less social mobility than comparable countries, and the effects of poverty still fall disproportionately on the young. We are deeply in thrall to individualism, says the report, and this hampers our capacity really to put ourselves at the service of the growth and safety of the new generation.

In short, this report is telling us that adults have to change if children are to be better cared for and their welfare better secured. But there are no simple scapegoats here, as if targeting one particular group for blame would help us move on. A good example is what is said here about working parents. It may be tempting to say that the root of many problems lies in the fact that too many mothers of small children are in regular employment and to suggest that the solution lies in a return to what is fondly imagined to be the traditional domestic pattern. But while there are undoubtedly some negative effects for children of being in group childcare, the two salient issues identified are, first, what we take for granted about work itself – both in terms of our attitudes to our own careers and in terms of what working patterns are encouraged by employers – and second, what kind of supplementary care is available when parents are working. Group childcare is not the only option: families, networks of friends or neighbours, informal associations, actually take up a good deal of the requirement here (as in fact they have done in more 'traditional' cultural contexts), and fewer negative results are visible.

But what this does is to focus our attention on the context in which child-rearing is happening. If we live in an environment where employers are habitually insensitive to family issues and needs, or in an environment where parents have not had the chance to build up networks of support, then the family with two working parents will be running some risks. If we do not want to run those risks, a good many things will have to change in attitudes and policies.

There are two striking aspects of the responses of many of the young people interviewed for this project which sharpen up this diagnosis further. The majority of these young people are passionately committed to the importance of friendship and keenly aware of the impact on their lives of family break-up (not least of the absence of a father). These concerns are in fact connected: children recognize that they need time and opportunity to work at their own relationships; and they suffer when adult relationships around them fail. The implication is that adults too need the time and freedom to work at sustaining relationships; but the climate we live in is not particularly friendly to this.

There is certainly no quick solution when we are speaking about a large-scale cultural phenomenon: laws cannot make marriages work. But what they can do is to give all reasonable support to men and women who want to be responsibly and generously there for their children, and who need to be helped to resist the sort of pressures that destroy relationships through overwork and economic hardship. Beyond this, we are in the territory of changing hearts. We need to develop a culture in which people are not only interested in their right to have a child but in how they guarantee the conditions in which a child can be brought up in security and emotional confidence. The report rightly stresses how essential it is that couples understand that their commitment to each other is absolutely bound up with the welfare of their children; so that working to secure that commitment is part of what is owed to those children. If we are serious about children's welfare, we need not only access to the right kind of training in parenting skills but a serious shared willingness as a society to educate young people about committed partnership, its importance and its challenges. In plain terms, it will not serve us as a society, and it will not serve the growing generation, if we simply regard marriage as just one option in the market-place of lifestyles. When this report argues for better and earlier sex education for our young people, it is not talking about an expanded curriculum of biological or even sociological instruction, or about the premature exposure of children to all the complexities of sexual practice. It is very specifically advocating a style of sex education that focuses on emotional maturity and self-awareness – with all that this means in terms of seeing this area of our lives in the context of adult and faithful responsibility.

So many aspects of this report bring us back to the same basic question. How can we raise confident, happy and creative human beings if we do not have some shared ideas about what human maturity and happiness look like? More sharply, how can we do this if we have no notion of what it is to 'educate our emotions'? The phrase is likely to be a rather unfamiliar one, sounding presumptuous or utopian or just authoritarian and bossy. But the truth is that when human beings act out their individual feelings without reflection and scrutiny, they are likely very soon to become incapable of living with each other; there is enough 'reality television' these days to provide dismally abundant evidence of this. And, that being said, it is interesting that another strand of reality TV has pointed up the issue from a different angle. 'The Monastery' initiated a succession of programmes in which an assortment of individuals spend time in an environment where a fixed rhythm of life combines with a critical scrutiny of passing feelings. It was made clear both how very hard we are likely to find it to see ourselves and our emotions from a bit of a distance, and how transforming and expanding it can be when we learn to do so. 'Educating' emotion is to do with this sort of patient realism about ourselves, with its corollary of empathy with others and patience with them as well.

Recent studies of childhood have underlined how the lack of dependable and loving parenting in the first years, even months, of life results in an emotional narrowing, an empathy deficit, which is very hard to overcome. It has been shown – by researchers such as Sue Gerhardt – that this involves a physiological dysfunction, where certain neural channels are never opened. The failure to engage with the independent psychological reality that is the child's consciousness because of a fixation on one's own needs replicates in the child the same incapacity to wait and to empathize, often with specially disastrous results in adolescence and early adulthood. The truth is that learning to see clearly one's own emotions and creating that element of distance from them is to create some space for the reality of a human other. Everyone except the most severely mentally disturbed learns a measure of this for their survival; the mature adult is the one who has made it an unobtrusive habit – and who, because of that, has some freedom to engage with and take responsibility for others.

Which is why, recalling the debate mentioned at the start of these reflections, tackling a poem with an emotionally challenging content in an environment where responsible adults are around to 'contain' some of the fallout is the opposite of irresponsible collusion with violence. When children are routinely exposed in the media to violence of word and action, without any mediation or analysis, it is bizarre that the literary representation of circumstances that could lead to violence should be so shocking to some. Leading a child to think through the feelings of another is not to assault the child's innocence or to normalize those feelings; it is to recognize (to stress the point once again) the intelligence of the child and to try and enlarge it so that he or she understands both their own feelings and those of others better – so that, perhaps, the child comes to see something of where the line is, in responsible human life, between experiencing passionate emotion and acting on it without thought. To deny the possibility of nourishing that sort of intelligence is to risk yet more uneducated emotion and reactive behaviour.

This report is not ashamed to put *love* at the centre of the child's needs – and the adult's too: love not as warm feeling alone, but as long-term commitment to someone else's well-being as something that matters profoundly to one's own well-being. That sort of commitment means relativizing your own sense of what you as an individual need, so as to discover what might be good for you *and* the other; and parenthood is one of the contexts where most people learn this most lastingly if they learn it at all. It does not guarantee happiness – the world is unpredictable and often cruel – but happiness has no chance without it, and when the cruel and unpredictable occurs, there will be more resources to meet it if love has been experienced.

The report is not a document of theology or even ethics; but it does force the reader to ask what we have in the 'bank' of mind and spirit in our culture that reinforces love and fidelity and offers some robust account of what long-term human welfare looks like and what it demands. The concern of all major religious communities with children and the family, and their heavy investment (not without controversy these days) in education, is sometimes taken to be essentially about indoctrination of children and control of sexuality (especially women's sexuality). The moral confusions and corruptions to which religious institutions, like others, are vulnerable have meant that these motivations have been very visible. But, to mention only the case of the Christian churches, there are deeper motivations, whose substance is relevant to plenty of people who may not share the doctrinal convictions of believers. Although this is an independent inquiry, it has been sponsored by The Children's Society with its roots firmly in the Church's life and vision. To the extent that it has worked out of these 'deeper motivations', it has shown clearly that they are acutely relevant to a wider public. Of those motivations, two are particularly important, and it is worth spelling out a little why this is so.

First, the basic texts of Christian faith contain some startling statements about children (even more startling two thousand years ago than now): the child is the one from whom the adult must learn about 'the Kingdom of God'; and the one who abuses or corrupts or deceives the child is destined for the harshest of judgements. The child not only has access to the Kingdom, s/he has a privileged place in it. This is not romantic speculation about children trailing clouds of glory, or even a celebration of childlike innocence. In its context, it seems to mean that it is the very powerlessness or vulnerability of the child that is important – important in securing their place of privilege, but also important as reminding the adult that receiving the news of the possibility of change, freedom, love, reconciliation, requires of the adult a degree of vulnerability and spontaneity that is normally overlaid by suspicion and self-defensiveness. And what is most damnable in human relationships is whatever pushes this to the margins or destroys it.

Second, there has been since the beginning of Christianity a conviction that faithful human relationship in marriage is a reflection of the faithfulness with which God relates to the universe and more specifically the faithfulness with which Jesus Christ relates to believers. In other words, the stable family unit when it is fully what it can be makes a statement about 'how things are' – about what cannot be shaken in a world where everything seems to be mobile and uncertain. It is true that the family can be a context of distraction from the truth, of limiting and unintelligent loyalty that blocks out the wider world – Jesus himself is brutally clear about this; but this does not alter what the family can be when it is animated by a love willing to grow beyond its own boundaries, a love confident enough not to be seeking for a retreat from a difficult larger world.

Two insights from the foundational texts of one religious faith which help explain why these issues matter to religious believers; other themes and motivations will no doubt be found in other faiths. But in our present context they highlight issues that are of the most urgent contemporary significance. The child is – among so much else – a sign of what is promised when we drop some of our obsession with defence and control; not in the name of some idealization of unthinking action but in the name of a willingness to be taught, to be nourished and to be surprised. And the committed family relationship is a sign, a statement of trust that there is something that cannot be invalidated or destroyed by any of the chances of the world, something of which our experience of committed love gives us a glimpse.

I said earlier that there are no quick solutions any more than there are any scapegoats in responding to the varied and sometimes troubling picture this report sketches for us. But if we are to respond intelligently to the intelligent observations of the young people whose experience has been at the heart of this work, we shall need to be aware of the resources we have for changing both policies and attitudes. This manifestly includes our heritage of religious belief. But to say this is also in the same moment to put the challenge to religious communities of all kinds as to their willingness to give the care and nurture of children the priority it deserves. There is more involved than simply defending the role of faith in education – and unless 'faith schools' show a keener than average awareness of some of the issues discussed above, they will be failing in a central aspect of their duty. There is more involved than the defence of traditional family patterns – unless believers can show all of us ways of handling the education of emotion and of preparing people for adult commitment in relationships, all that will be seen is an agenda of anxiety, censoriousness and repression. There is more involved than a generally welcoming attitude to the young – on its own, this can be felt as a patronizing attempt to hold on to unenthusiastic members.

The report asks for more from churches and religious communities – as it does from all kinds of bodies in our society. It asks for a coherent vision of how human beings grow and become capable of giving and deserving trust, for unremitting advocacy on behalf of those who are growing up in poverty, for a systematic willingness to pay attention to how children and young people actually talk about themselves, and perhaps above all for a realistic and grateful appreciation of who and what our young people really are. In a climate where the mixture of sentimentalism and panic makes discussion of children's issues so difficult, this report will bring a thoughtful and hopeful perspective. For the sake of the rising generation and their successors, I hope it will be welcomed and acted upon.

Members of the Inquiry Panel

Patron

The Most Revd and The Rt Hon. Dr Rowan Williams, Archbishop of Canterbury

Chair

Professor Judy Dunn, Professor of Developmental Psychology, Institute of Psychiatry, King's College London

Panel Members

- Professor Sir Albert Aynsley-Green, Children's Commissioner for England
- Dr Muhammad Abdul Bari, Secretary General, the Muslim Council of Britain
- Jim Davis, Programme Manager, Children's Participation Project Wessex, The Children's Society
- Professor Philip Graham, Emeritus Professor of Child Psychiatry, Institute of Child Health, London
- Professor Kathleen Kiernan, Professor of Social Policy and Demography, University of York

Acknowledgements

The idea of *A Good Childhood* has been at the heart of The Children's Society for nearly a decade, and hundreds of people have been involved in bringing it into being. Their vision and commitment has not only produced this book, but also helps children and young people across the UK every day.

We are grateful to all those who supported the inquiry with advice and encouragement during its development stage, particularly to Caroline Abrahams, Henrietta Bond, Dr Marcia Brophy, Isabel Carter, Christopher Cloke, Ian Hargreaves, Lord Laming, Dr Ann Morisy, Rachel O'Brien, Helen Patterson, Steve Pearce, David Rayner, Revd Angus Ritchie, Professor Sir Michael Rutter, Professor Adrian Thatcher and Michael Williams; and to steering group members Sue Burridge, Jenny Driscoll, David Evans, The Rt Revd Bishop Tim Stevens, Dr Keith White and William Wilks. Our gratitude also to those charitable trusts who supported the inquiry: Allchurches Trust, Gulbenkian Foundation and PF Charitable Trust.

We were overwhelmed by the thousands of people who sent in evidence to the inquiry, and tremendously grateful to all those who shared their views and experiences as parents and grandparents, carers and care workers, teachers, academics and professionals. A deep concern for children's lives today shone through every submission. It's impossible to acknowledge every submission by name, and so this list simply acknowledges those organizations that responded to our call for evidence. We're grateful to them for sharing their expertise and experience: Act 4, Action for Prisoners' Families, Active Training and Education Trust, Alcohelp Charity, Alone in London Service, Anorexia and Bulimia Care, Association for Family Therapy, Association of Catholic Women, Association of Child Psychotherapists, Association of School and College Leaders, Association of Young People with ME, Baptist Union of Great Britain, Barnardo's, BIBIC, Blue Balloon Foundation, British Association of Community Child Health, British Association of Social Workers, British Humanist Association, Brook, BT Better World Campaign, Care Co-ordination Network UK, CAVI, Centre for Child Mental Health, Centre for Crime and Justice Studies at King's College London, CfBT Education Trust, Charlie Waller Memorial Trust, Child Bereavement Network, Child Poverty Action Group, Childhood First, Children's Links, Children in Scotland, Children's Trust Tadworth, ChildWise, Churches Network for Non-violence, Citizen's Income Trust, Commission for Racial Equality, Comprehensive Future, Connexions – Humber, Contact a Family, Dauntsey's School Wiltshire, Daycare Trust, Diocese of Southwell and Nottingham, Early Childhood Forum, Early Education, Economics and Business Education Association, Entertainment and Leisure Software Publishers Association, Envision, Family Education Trust,

Family Links, Family Policy Alliance, Federation of Children's Book Groups, Food Standards Agency, Fostering Network, Full Time Mothers, Girlguiding UK, Global Initiative to End All Corporal Punishment, G-Nostics, Hertfordshire's Children's Trust Partnership, Home-Start UK, Hope UK, Housing Justice, Human Scale Education, I CAN, Independent Care After Incest and Rape, Ironduke Theatre, Jehovah's Witnesses, Kids, Learning Space, Leckhampton After School Club, Lewisham YOT, Limehurst High School Leicestershire, Maranatha Community, Matson Neighbourhood Project, Media March, MENCAP, Mental Health Foundation, Moorthorpe Children's Centre, National Association of Head Teachers, National Children's Bureau, National Consumer Council, National Heart Forum, National Literacy Trust, National Pyramid Trust for Children, National Union of Teachers, National Youth Agency, New Economics Foundation, Newcastle College, Norland College, Northumberland County Council, Nurture Group Network, Parents Returning into Meaningful Education, Parenting Education and Support Forum, Parentline Plus, Pimlico School London, Play England, Polka Theatre, Pre-school Learning Alliance, QA Research, Refuge, Relationships Foundation, Romanian Child Action, RoSPA, Royal College of Midwives, Salvation Army, Save Kids TV, Save the Children, Schools Out, Scouts, Scripture Union, Sex Education Forum, Shelter, SkillsActive, Spurgeon's Child Care, St John's Wood Adventure Playground, Stonewall, St Thomas's Church, Ashton-in-Makerfield CYFA group, Sure Start Rosehill, Sustainable Development

Commission, Synectics Education Initiative, Teens in Crisis, Torbay Play Forum, Toynbee School Hampshire, Turtle Key Arts Trust, Victim Support, Wellington College Berkshire, What About the Children?, Wildlife Trust, Winston's Wish, Worcester College of Technology, Working Families, www.talk2me.org.uk and YWCA.

The illustrations in this book were kindly sent in by children and young people in response to our call for evidence in 2006 and 2007. Because these submissions were anonymous we could not trace the senders to notify them of publication. If you or your child are the author of one of these works and would like to be credited in future editions, please contact The Children's Society.

The panel was greatly helped by a number of academics and experts who generously gave their time to the inquiry, preparing papers for the panel or presenting at panel meetings. For this we're indebted to William Atkinson, Head Teacher of Phoenix High School, London; Dr Stephan Collishaw, Institute of Psychiatry, King's College London; Neil Hawkes of Values Education; Dr Sajid Humayun, Institute of Psychiatry, King's College London; Ed Mayo, Chief Executive of the British National Consumer Council; Dr Agnes Nairn, University of Bath; Professor Iram Siraj-Blatchford, Institute of Education, University of London; Professor Peter Smith, Goldsmith's College, University of London; and especially to Professor Melanie Killen, University of Maryland and to Professor Jonathan Bradshaw of the University of York. The panel was also honoured to meet Patricia Lewsley, Northern Ireland's Commissioner for Children and

Young People; Kathleen Marshall, Scotland's Commissioner for Children and Young People; and Professor Sheila Greene of Trinity University Dublin, who each represented the experience of children and young people in their jurisdictions with great passion.

Many others helped the inquiry team to prepare briefing papers for the panel, or provided specialist advice. For their generosity and expertise we'd like to thank Camila Batmanghelidjh, Kids Company; Gill Frances, NCB; Professor Robert Goodman, Institute of Psychiatry; Professor Ian Goodyer, University of Cambridge; Tara McKearney; Ofcom; Professor Pam Sammons, University of Nottingham; The Sustainable Development Commission; head teacher Eugene Symonds and the pupils of West Kidlington School, Oxfordshire; and translators Huw Tegid and Bethan Wyn-Jones.

We were delighted when Professor Richard Layard suggested a series of seminars on child well-being at the London School of Economics and are very grateful to him and to all those who took part for the lively and insightful discussions. For their fascinating presentations our thanks go to Dr Robin Banerjee, University of Sussex; Professor Jay Belsky, Birkbeck College; Professor John Ermisch, University of Essex; Professor Philip Graham, Institute of Child Health; Professor Paul Gregg, University of Bristol; Professor Kathleen Kiernan, University of York; Professor Melanie Killen, University of Maryland; Professor Sonia Livingstone, London School of Economics; Professor Steven Machin, University College London; Professor Barbara Maughan, Institute of Psychiatry; Professor Peter Mortimore, Institute of Education; and Professor Stephen Scott, Institute of Psychiatry.

At each theme meeting the inquiry panel was joined by a group of children and young people who brought the evidence to life by sharing their own experiences. For this we'd like to thank Lesley Collard, Aadam Gasmi, Amy Hyam, Mark Williams and Mathew Taggart of High Close School, Wokingham, together with Anna Frazer and Nikkie Mann; Brennan Balmer, Eleri Evans, Kelly Jack, Richard Manning and Tamara Sucic of Pembroke School, Pembroke, together with Chris Rigby and Kathryn Warder; Holly Prentise, Dennis Ramm and JoJo Roberts of Thanet Community Development Project, Ramsgate, together with Donna Ramm and Ann Rayment; Fabbiha Chowdhury and Noshin Chowdhury of The Children's Voice Project, Bethnal Green, together with Yasmin Haque and Veronika Neyer; Gary Buchanan, Marie Buchanan, Jennifer Hart and Heather Turnbull of Scotland's Commissioner for Children and Young People's Health Advisory Group, together with Stephen Bermingham and Gillian Munro; Megan O'Kane and Vishal Sridhar of the Northern Ireland Commissioner for Children and Young People's Youth Panel, together with Marlene Kinghan and Ken Smyth; Adam Green and Jamie McKay of West Sussex PAR, together with Emma Sweatman; and Sean Crannage, Jason Hackett and Rebecca Hunter of Youth Justice North East, together with Mohammed Ali and Peter Lowe.

To ensure that the panel heard from particular groups

of children and young people who may not have participated in the inquiry in other ways The Children's Society organized a series of focus groups that included underfives, refugee and asylum-seeking children, rroma children, young offenders and children and young people in secure estates, looked-after children, those excluded from school, black and minority ethnic girls, one-parent families, disabled children, and children who had been affected by domestic violence. We are very grateful to Aberlour's Pollok Young People's Project, Barton Moss Secure Training Centre, Baytree Centre, Beacon Centre for the Blind, Beever Primary School, Canterbury Nursery School, Cardiff Young People First, Hammersmith and Fulham Action on Disability's First Chance Project, Her Majesty's Young Offenders Institutions Feltham and Werrington House, Lister Community School, Llandeyrn Play Centre, NCB Northern Ireland, Norwich International Youth Project, One Parent Families, Gingerbread, Porlock Hall Pupil Referral Unit and Wolverley Church of England Secondary School.

We'd also like to say a special thank-you to the BBC Newsround team, whose partnership with the inquiry helped us to hear the views of thousands more children nationwide.

The work of the Most Revd and The Rt Hon. the Lord Archbishop of Canterbury, Dr Rowan Williams, helped to shape the inquiry from the beginning, and we are honoured that he agreed to serve as patron of The Good Childhood Inquiry and hosted a panel meeting at Lambeth Palace. The Children's Society has enjoyed the support of the Church of England for many years, and we're grateful to staff at Lambeth Palace, and to members of the Archbishops' Council and officers from the Mission and Public Affairs, Education and Communications Divisions for the Church of England, Church House, London, for their ongoing support, as well as to Diocesan Children's and Youth Work Advisers and all those committed individuals and parishes who sent in evidence to the inquiry. In the autumn of 2007 we were honoured to partner in a series of stimulating public debates on childhood in St Paul's Cathedral, London, for which we are indebted to Canon Edmund Newell and Elizabeth Foy at St Paul's Institute.

The inquiry panel met at 11 Million, the office of the Children's Commissioner for England, and our thanks go to all those who made us so welcome there. For their professionalism and enthusiasm we thank Anni Barry and Marion O'Brien at the Centre for Economic Performance at the London School of Economics, who patiently prepared the manuscript of this report. For their vision and encouragement to The Children's Society in this new venture, a special thank-you to agent Caroline Dawnay of United Agents, and Stuart Proffitt, our editor at Penguin.

Hundreds of volunteers, staff and trustees from The Children's Society supported The Good Childhood Inquiry over the years, and it would be impossible to name them all. But the inquiry is especially grateful to Esther Hughes (Head of the inquiry team) and to Larissa Pople (its Policy and Research Officer), who worked tirelessly throughout the inquiry and whose dedication was vital to its success. We are also grateful to Campaigns and Media Officer Zoë Mason and Administrators Rachel Sharp and Saraya Afolabi, who deserve a very special note of thanks. The team's professionalism and devotion to the inquiry was instrumental in the production of this report. I would also like to recognize the important contribution that Penny Nicholls and Gwyther Rees made in the preparations for the panel meetings. Finally, we are grateful to interns Ashley Brothers and Chris Gibbons, researchers Lucy Bowes, Catherine McCarthy and Fiona Mitchell, and funding consultant Elaine Banna.

We opened this acknowledgement by saying that the idea of *A Good Childhood* has been at the heart of The Children's Society for nearly a decade. It is important to recognize the origins of the idea, which came from Helen Goodman MP, who at the time was Head of Planning in our organization, and the support she received from Ian Sparks, the then Chief Executive. Finally, I want to thank all The Children's Society's projects, and the children and young people we work with, for their contributions to the inquiry. It is the voice of these children and young people, and their vision of a good childhood, which is at the centre of all our work.

Bob Reitemeier
Chief Executive, The Children's Society
November 2008

Notes

Chapter 1: Is There a Problem?

1. ChildWise (2006).
2. Park et al. (2004), Section 4.6.
3. Collishaw et al. (2004) and Green et al. (2005). The first paper covers 1974, 1986 and 1999 and uses standard sets of questions asked of parents, using closely comparable questions in each survey. For each type of problem, the cut-off score for 'significant problems' is inevitably arbitrary, but it is comparable in all the surveys.

The second paper compares the results of identical ONS surveys of child psychiatric morbidity in 1999 and 2004, which showed no change between the two years in either type of problem (see Green et al., 2005: 8); so for 1999 and 2004 the figure in the text shows the same values in both years.

4. West and Sweeting (2003). Compares 1987 and 1999. In addition, preliminary results for Britain from the 2006 Youth Trends Survey supplied by Stephan Collishaw provide further evidence of increased emotional problems between 1986 and 2006.
5. UNICEF (2007).
6. Based mainly on WHO (2008) and relates mainly to 2005/6. The third column is the unweighted average of seventeen European countries not formerly members of the Soviet bloc. The income data for the USA are from the Luxembourg Income Study (2004) and the European data from Eurostat (2006 data). We are grateful for the help of Dominic Richardson at OECD.
7. See Chapter 8.
8. Joseph Rowntree Foundation (2008).
9. Some people argue that present levels of individualism are needed to maximize the GDP. But happiness depends on human relationships as well as GDP, and the evidence suggests that better relationships would outweigh

in value any consequent loss of GDP. (Layard, 2005). See also Chapter 8 below.

10. Hofstede (2000).

11. Municipal Museum, Istanbul. Information from David Piachaud.

12. Layard (2005: 81).

13. Children's Society (2008a). Representative sample of over 1,000 UK adults surveyed by telephone in January 2007. See also Park et al. (2004: 41–2).

14. Putnam (2000: 140). For continental Europe we have shorter time-series but do not observe the same fall in trust.

15. Youth Survey of the British Household Panel Survey, 2006.

16. The genetic contribution to cooperative behaviour is well-documented, see Wright (1994).

17. www.childrenssociety.org.uk.

18. On these topics see HM Treasury and DfES (2007b); Equalities Review (2008); HM Treasury and DfES (2007a); Sloper et al. (2007); Platt (2007); Mills (2004).

19. DCSF (2007).

Chapter 2: Family

20. Gregg et al. (2005).

21. Ellwood and Jencks (2004); Lord Chancellor's Department (1999), p. 3.

22. Bowlby (1969); Rutter et al. (2008b).

23. Ainsworth et al. (1978).

24. Baumrind (1971).

25. Plomin (1990).

26. Dunn et al. (1991).

27. Burgess (2007); Lewis and Lamb (2006).

28. Flouri (2005).

29. Pleck and Masciadrelli (2004); Lewis and Lamb (2006).

30. O'Brien (2005).

31. Scott (2004).

32. Grossman et al. (2002).

33. Lewis and Lamb (2006).

34. Flouri and Buchanan (2002).

35. Lewis and Lamb (2006).

36. Children's Society (2008a).

37. In the UK the EPPE study (Effective Provision of Pre-school Education) and the ALSPAC study (Avon Longitudinal Study of Parents and Children); in the USA the NICHD study (National Institute of Child Health and Human Development).

38. Belsky et al. (2007).

39. Sylva et al. (2004).

40. Sammons et al. (2004).

41. Sammons et al. (2007).

42. It is found in NICHD (2003) and Gregg et al. (2007), which is based on ALSPAC. It is not found in Sammons et al. (2007), which is based on EPPE.

43. Dmitrieva et al. (2007).

44. Dunn et al. (2006).

45. Baumrind (1971).

46. NFPI (2000).

47. Kiernan and Mensah (2008).

48. Amato and Keith (1991); Pryor and Rodgers (2001).

49. Clarke-Stewart and Brentano (2006).

50. Lamb et al. (1999).

51. Amato (1995).

52. Cherlin et al. (1991); Elliott and Richards (1991).

53. Pleck and Masciadrelli (2004).

54. Dunn (2003).

55. Maclean and Eekelaar (1995).

56. Blackwell and Dawe (2003).

57. Jaffee et al. (2003).

58. Dunn and Deater-Deckard (2001); Lussier et al. (2002).

59. Buchanan (2008); Dunn et al. (2006).

60. Relationships between children and their grandparents are of course closer the closer the relationship between their mother and the grandparents (Bridges et al., 2007).

61. Ford et al. (2004).

62. McLanahan and Sandefur (1994) give evidence for a high figure for the USA. Ford et al. (2004) give evidence for a lower one for England.

63. Analysis of the Millennium Cohort Study for the Good Childhood Inquiry. Very similar findings are found in the large survey in the West Country (ALSPAC).

64. Dunn et al. (2005).

65. Kiernan and Smith (2003).

66. Kiernan (2004).

67. In Britain we have data on the percentage of married people who consider theirs a 'happy relationship'. For those aged 33 in 1991 it was 81 per cent, and for those aged 30 in 2000 it was 64 per cent. Men and women gave virtually the same answers. See Ferri et al. (2003), table 4.1.

68. The evidence suggests that this can be experienced equally through the love of two parents of different or the same gender (Golombok, 2002 and 2006).

69. Parenting support and education is already an explicit priority for Children's Services, and should continue to be so.

70. The cost would be about £150 per ceremony, or £40 million a year if a quarter of a million births were celebrated in this way.

71. For a detailed analysis of leave entitlements in different countries see Moss and Deven (2006).

72. The Childcare Act 2006 introduced a new framework for the provision of childcare in England and Wales that goes some way towards achieving this.

73. An excellent book of helpful advice for parents who split up is Woodall and Woodall (2007).

Chapter 3: Friends

74. Schaffer (2004).

75. Children's Society (2006).

76. Loehlin (1992); Manke et al. (1995); Pike and Atzaba-Poria (2003).

77. Data supplied by Stephan Collishaw based on the age 16 follow-up of the 1970 British Cohort Study and new data collected for 16-year-olds in the 2006 Youth Trends Study.

78. Howes (1988) and Howes et al. (1992).

79. Dunn (2004).

80. Dunn et al. (1995); Dunn et al. (2000).

81. Berndt et al. (1999).

82. Pelkonen et al. (2003).

83. Field (1984).

84. Goodyer et al. (1989).

85. Kramer and Gottman (1992); Ladd (1999).

86. Hodges and Perry (1999).

87. Newson and Newson (1970).

88. Gottman (1986).

89. Woodward and Fergusson (1999); Arseneault et al. (2006).

90. This phrase is from Palmer (2006).

91. Children's Society (2008a).

92. Gill (2007).

93. ibid., p. 49.

94. Home Office Statistics. England and Wales. See Povey et al. (2008).

95. Madge and Barker (2007).

96. Gill (2007).

97. DCSF (2007).

98. 86 per cent of children now do two hours of school sport a week.

99. Make Space Youth Review (2007).

100. ibid.

101. MORI (2002).

102. Make Space Youth Review (2007). See also Feinstein et al. (2005) and Robson and Feinstein (2007).

103. Udry (2003).

104. Collins (2003).

105. Wellings et al. (1994). For last row see Wellings et al. (2001).

106. Wellings et al. (1994), Table 2.7.

107. 99 per cent. Wellings et al. (1994), p. 72.

108. Ingham (1998).

109. Wight et al. (2000) surveyed all 13 to 14-year-olds in an area of East Scotland. Of those who had had sex, 45 per cent of girls and 32 per cent of boys said it had happened too early or should not have happened at all. See also Rundle et al. (2008).

110. Social Exclusion Unit (1999).

111. Ingham (1998).

112. Smith and Shu (2000).

113. Survey in Leicestershire by Rob Osborn.

114. Noret and Rivers (2006). See also Smith et al. (2008).

115. See UNICEF (2007). The exception is Sweden where bullying is much less common.

116. Smith et al. (2003). See also Olweus (1993) and Smith et al. (2004).

117. Hartup and Abecassis (2004).

118. Newburn (2007), Fig. 18.7. Based on the Home Office's Crime and Justice Survey of households, which covers younger age groups than their regular British Crime Survey. Both are surveys of the experience of being a victim.

119. Newburn (2007), Fig. 18.2. Based on the Home Office's infrequent self-report survey on committing offences.

120. The main data on criminal activity come from the British Crime Survey of victimization. This of course does not identify the age of the offender. But there are periodic surveys of self-reported offending on which the remarks are based. (For the population as a whole the experience of violent crime by offenders of all ages has been falling.) See also Home Office (2008).

121. The government's current objective is one per constituency, which is rather fewer than we recommend.

122. One model of a youth centre for a very disadvantaged community is the Kids Company drop-in centre in Camberwell.

123. Smith et al. (2004).

124. The government issued guidance on sex and relationships education within the PHSE curriculum in 2000, which sets out clearly that it should recognize the importance of love and care and responsibilities as well as sex.

Chapter 4: Lifestyle

125. Thanks to Professor Sonia Livingstone for this quotation.

126. ONS Time Use Survey 2001. Around 1,000 children. Data on 'primary activity'. Analysis kindly provided by Professor J. Gershuny of Oxford University. Remarks about changes since 1975 based on his comparison with the BBC Audience Research Department's Time Use Survey in 1975 which was a highly comparable diary study. The comparison also revealed that conversation had halved since 1975 but travel had doubled (some of which could be with the family).

127. The data on television watching and Internet use in 2001 are broadly consistent with those for 2006 in Ofcom (2006), which show that children aged 8–15 spent 14 hours watching television per week and three and a half hours using the Internet (including computer games).

128. Childwise (2006).

129. Balding (2007).

130. Hollis (2002).

131. For most of the above see Webley et al. (2001).

132. Schor (1998).

133. Children's Society (2008a).

134. Schor (2004), p. 179.

135. Fielder et al. (2007).

136. Layard (2005: 88–90).

137. Schor (2004). This suggests rather than demonstrates causality.

138. A child who moves up one percentile point in the ladder of media use will move up 0.12 points in the ladder of mental ill health.

139. Nairn and Ormond (2007). See also Kasser (2002). In Britain Agnes Nairn and her colleagues have studied 9 to 13-year-olds in six schools in different parts of the country. They found that children who were more materialistic had a lower opinion of their parents and, more seriously, lower self-esteem.

140. For details of the Radio and Television Act (1996: 844) see www.rtvv.se. The effectiveness of the law is limited in two ways. The ban relates to advertising around programmes directed at children (rather than all advertising aimed at children) and it does not cover advertising coming from outside the country by satellite or other methods.

141. Millwood Hargrave and Livingstone (2006); Browne and Hamilton-Giachritis (2005); Layard (2005: 87). All methods have their problems but the cumulative lesson is clear.

142. Livingstone (2008).

143. For a vigorous defence of videogames see Chatfield (2008).

144. Reported in Anderson et al. (2007: 143).

145. Byron (2008). This also covered videogames, and concluded that there was a lack of direct evidence about their effects.

146. For parents the Internet is harder to supervise than television (except in terms of time spent on the computer). Three-quarters of parents have rules about television and DVD watching.

147. Some 300 research projects in 21 countries have studied Internet use by teenagers. Their finding is that, among online teenagers, 20–30 per cent have seen violent, gruesome or hate sites, 20 per cent have experienced online bullying or hostility, and 10 per cent have sent such hostile messages (Livingstone, 2007). Further, 30–40 per cent have seen online pornography; between 10 and 40 per cent have gone to a meeting with someone they met online; and similar proportions have been sexually harassed online. An online Dutch survey reported that around half of online teens had been asked to undress on webcam (Pardoen and Pijpers, 2006).

148. See Seawell (1998). The evidence suggests that inappropriate sexual content is mainly dangerous when linked to violence (Millwood Hargrave and Livingstone, 2006).

149. Singleton et al. (2001: 18, 45, 48).

150. Marsden et al. (2005).

151. Balding (2007: 60).

152. The recommended daily limits are 4 units for men and 3 for women. A unit equals a small glass of wine or equivalent alcohol content.

153. Wells et al. (2006). See also Strategy Unit (2004).

154. Singleton et al. (2001).

155. Academy of Medical Sciences (2004).

156. Turning Point (2006).

157. Advisory Council on the Misuse of Drugs (2007) and their 2003 report.

158. Dependence here means *either* everyday use for at least two weeks *or* felt dependence *or* inability to cut down *or* need for ever larger amounts *or* withdrawal symptoms. The figure is for 16 to 19-year-olds (Singleton et al., 2001).

159. Moore et al. (2007).

160. Fuller (2008). Data for 15-year-olds.

161. See for example Runciman (2000). The Royal College of Psychiatrists (2000) estimate that a half of all crime is drug-related. This includes crimes committed in order to pay for drugs.

162. ONS, Social Trends (2008: 98–9).

163. Department of Health Survey.

164. On this paragraph see Department of Health (2004). See also Reilly et al. (2003). The effects of moderate and extreme obesity on Type 2 diabetes, osteoarthritis and heart disease are firmly established.

165. McCormick and Stone (2006).

166. The number of children going to school by car has doubled over the past twenty years with a corresponding decrease in walking and cycling to school (Department of Health, 2004: 60).

167. Even if the most modern videogames involve the use of energy, it is minimal compared with the energy used in sport.

168. This has been improving slightly in recent years. See SHEU (2004) and Balding (2007).

169. Mintel, *Children's Eating Habits*, 2003, quoted in NFPI (2004).

170. ONS (2000).

171. NFPI (2004).

172. Fuller (2008). 19 per cent of girls and 12 per cent of boys.

173. Balding (2007: 66).

174. ONS (2005).

175. Bonell et al. (2007). For the ineffectiveness of direct policies see their references 4–7 and, on sex education, Graham et al. (2002) and Henderson et al. (2007). The effect of school ethos emerged from a naturalistic study of health behaviours in Scotland, and from randomized control trials in the Aban Aya project in Chicago (12 schools) and in the Gatehouse project in Australia (22 schools). See also Rutter et al. (1979) and Mortimore et al. (1988).

176. The government is currently conducting a review into the effects of commercialization upon children.

Chapter 5: Values

177. Lyubomirsky (2007), chapter 5.

178. Eisenberg and Faber (1998); Zahn-Wexler et al. (1992). Parallel evidence for the genetic contribution to the variance in psychopathology is also accumulating; see Viding et al. (2008).

179. Ridley (1996).

180. Baumrind (1991); Grusec (2006).

181. Dunn (2004).

182. Reported by Melanie Killen.

183. Coie and Dodge (1998).

184. Reported by Melanie Killen.

185. Killen et al. (2006).

186. 2003 data. Park et al. (2004). Similarly many fewer young people think the courts are prejudiced than did so in 1994.

187. Lovat and Toomey (2007); Farrer (2000). Another important initiative is the UNICEF Rights Respecting Schools initiative (see www.unicef. org.uk). For a preliminary evaluation see Covell and Howe (2005).

188. Davidson and Harrington (2002).

189. Goleman (1995).

190. Reivich et al. (2005).

191. Weissberg (2007).

192. As we point out in Chapter 6, there needs to be a whole-school

approach, supplemented by specific teaching of life skills (see Weare, 2000 and Weare and Gray, 2003).

193. Some schools use up to two hours.

194. See for example the huge collection of materials assembled in the USA by CASEL (the Collaborative for Academic, Social and Emotional Learning) at CASEL.org.

195. Hall (1999) and, on the USA, Putnam (2000). See also Halpern (2004).

196. This does not mean that every uplifting experience is necessarily good. Neither belonging to the Hitler youth nor taking drugs is good – in both cases the consequences are terrible.

197. Frankl (2004).

198. Since 2006 schools have had a duty to promote the broader well-being of pupils.

199. For evidence on the psychological benefits to the volunteers see Meier and Stutzer (2008).

Chapter 6: Schooling

200. Sammons et al. (2008b), Table 2.4.

201. Prais (1995), Chapter 5; OECD (2008), Chapter 1 and Table 1.2.

202. Figures from DCSF.

203. Machin and McNally (2008).

204. Burroughs-Lange (2006). 'This study of 42 primary schools serving disadvantaged areas in 10 London boroughs showed that very little progress in literacy was made by children who commenced Year 1 as the lowest achievers in their classes. The exception was for children who received Reading Recovery intervention during the year. These Reading Recovery children, who had entry levels similar to comparison children in schools without Reading Recovery, had, by the end of the year, on average gained 20 months on word reading age.' On mathematics recovery see the report of the committee chaired by Sir Peter Williams (Williams, 2008).

205. This and the following analyses are by Sandra McNally based on LEASIS and school performance tables. Free school meals data are for all the children in each school. All figures in the tables are unweighted averages across schools.

206. On this paragraph see Sammons et al. (2006, 2008a). Causality here is complicated. On average children on free school meals show lower attainment and worse behaviour at all ages, and they also cause other children to perform and behave worse.

207. Dolton and Newsom (2003) found that in six Inner London boroughs, the annual turnover rate was 27 per cent in the most deprived quarter of schools, compared with around 18 per cent elsewhere. This difference was shown to influence school performance.

208. Scheerens and Bosker (1997).

209. McKinsey and Company (2007), p. 34. The analysis charts for each country the percentage of the variance of 15-year-old student performance due to student background against the average PISA score. They are closely correlated.

210. OECD (2007), Executive Summary, Tables 4 and 5. With Germany, we were above average in science (Table 2).

211. OECD (1995) based on IALS.

212. Steedman et al. (2004). Data for 2003.

213. See the website of the European Centre for the Development of Vocational Training (CEDEFOP) http://www.trainingvillage.gr/etv/ information_resources/nationalVet/thematic/.

214. DfES, First Release SFR 22/2007. Data for England.

215. McKinsey and Company (2007).

216. Sanders and Rivers (1996).

217. Day et al. (2004). See also Hattie (2003) and Blatchford et al. (2002).

218. Nickell and Quintini (2002) show that between 1975–9 and 1985–9 male teachers' pay fell by 10 percentile points in the pay distribution. Correspondingly, between 1979 and 1991 the test scores (when tested at 11) of men entering teaching also fell by 10 percentile points.

219. See Education and Skills Act, 2008 and DIUS and DCSF (2008). See also DCSF Press Notice on School Report Cards of 14 October 2008.

220. At 'Level 1' literacy and numeracy.

221. Noden and West (2008).

222. Hall and Øzerk (2008), pp. 18–19.

223. The data on each school are constructed and published by DCSF from individual pupil records. They show (i) unadjusted scores (averages and percentages above a cut-off), and (ii) 'contextual' value-added scores for 7–11 and 11–14, adjusting for pupils' backgrounds. The schools appear in alphabetical order within each LEA. But many newspapers print league tables based on unadjusted scores (usually percentage above a cut-off) ranked in order of their score. The BBC website also ranks schools, but by value-added scores.

224. The numbers getting five A*–Cs in any subject were 60.8 per cent in 2007.

225. For evidence of the poor effects of teaching to the test see Glewwe et al. (2002) and the review by Harlen and Deakin Crick (2002), who report that 'When passing tests is high stakes, teachers adopt a teaching style which emphasises transmission teaching of knowledge, thereby favouring those students who prefer to learn in this way and disadvantaging and lowering the self-esteem of those who prefer more active and creative learning experiences. High-stakes tests can become the rationale for all that is done in classrooms, permeating teacher-initiated assessment interactions. Students are aware of a performance ethos in the classroom and that the tests give only a narrow view of what they can do. Students dislike high-stakes tests, show high levels of test anxiety (particularly girls) and prefer other forms of assessment.'

226. Davies and Brember (1998, 1999).

227. Of 15-year-olds in England, 65 per cent report that they feel pressured by schoolwork. This is the highest level among 41 countries in Europe and North America (except Wales and Portugal). The unweighted average for all these countries is 45 per cent; see Currie et al. (2008). See also McDonald (2001) on the findings for primary school children.

228. Mortimore (2007).

229. DCSF (2007), p. 67. A level normally corresponds to two years' work.

230. Sammons et al. (2008a).

231. Wilson et al. (2007). Covers London and other metropolitan areas.

232. Neill (2008).

233. Weare (2000) and Weare and Gray (2003).

234. For the case for screening see Friedman (2006).

235. We have in mind something like a modified version of the Strengths and Difficulties Questionnaires. At age 5 this would replace the existing rather limited range of questions on which the current teacher-based profile is based.

Chapter 7: Mental Health

236. Green et al. (2005). This excludes educational psychologists who are mainly providing assessment.

237. Our earlier proposals are listed on page 31.

238. Green et al. (2005). The following table is based on their Table 4.1.

239. Moffitt (1993).

240. See Green et al. (2005, p. xxi), which compares the two ONS surveys, using the diagnostic categories shown in Table 1. A separate analysis of the SDQ ratings in the survey suggested some slight improvement over the period (Maughan et al., 2008).

241. Also, for young people aged 16–19 the proportions who were mentally ill rose from 10 per cent to 14 per cent between 1993 and 2000 (see Singleton et al., 2001), though these figures are subject to sampling error.

242. Plomin (1990).

243. Ford et al. (2004), Table 5. Neither parental income, social class, quality of school or living in a deprived neighbourhood were found to have any direct effect on child mental health – or changes in child mental health (Ford et al., 2007a, Table 3).

244. ibid.

245. Scott et al. (2001), p.1.

246. Fergusson et al. (2005), Table 1. Data for Christchurch, New Zealand. Even if other influences on subsequent outcomes are taken into account, the effect of childhood conduct disorder remains very strong (see their Table 3).

247. The child mental health services comprise four tiers, which are, broadly speaking:

Tier 1. Universal services (schools, GP practices, social care).

Tier 2. Specialist individual professionals relating closely to primary care.

Tier 3. Specialist multi-disciplinary teams (secondary care).

Tier 4. Tertiary care.

See National Service Framework for Children, Young People and Maternity Services, Standard 9.

248. In some cases, especially ADHD, medication may be recommended.

249. Fonagy et al. (2002). This does not deny that psychoanalytic thinking has contributed greatly to the development of a listening culture.

250. A typical size of effect is 0.6 standard deviations, which is sufficient to raise someone from the 5th percentile to the 15th percentile.

251. See for example Lochman and Pardini, 'Cognitive-Behavioral Thera-pies', in Rutter et al. (2008b), pp. 1026–45. For other basic texts see Turk, Graham and Verhulst (2007) and Goodman and Scott (2005).

252. For example, The Triple P (Positive Parenting Programme) from Australia and the Incredible Years Programme from the US – see Sanders et al. (2003) and Webster-Stratton et al. (1989). The Triple P parenting programme is organized at five levels. Level one is universal information, delivered though radio and television shows. Level two is two twenty-minute consultations by, say, a nurse in a general practice, while level three comprises four forty-minute consultations for somewhat more difficult problems. Level four consists of an eight-week programme of consultations once a week for an hour or more, and finally, for those who have additional problems, level five adds specific modules addressing issues such as inter-parental relationship difficulties, or depression.

The Incredible Years programme is a twelve-week parenting programme including videotape clips of parents behaving in a range of ways with their children. The content initially covers promotion of desirable behaviour through play (three weeks), then moves to praise and rewards (three weeks). Then it covers the handling of misbehaviour, including ignoring minor misbehaviour (two weeks), using negative consequences (two weeks) and sending children to 'time-out' (two weeks). Most commonly through detailed group discussion and role play, the parental behaviour that leads to better child behaviour is drawn out and practised. The programme can also be done individually, with or without the children.

253. Scott (2005).

254. Current policies can be found in Standard 9 of the National Service Framework for Children, Young People and Maternity Services (Department of Health and Department for Education and Skills, 2004). See also *Every Child Matters* (DfES, 2004) and *The Children's Plan* (DCSF, 2007). At the time of writing an official CAMHS Review was in progress.

255. For a summary of effective treatments see Wolpert et al. (2006).

256. See Layard (2008).

257. Department of Health (2008).

258. The typical therapy course would be one year on full pay with two days off-the-job training and three days on the job in a service providing NICE-recommended treatments.

259. Employing 1,000 extra therapists would cost around £50 million, but some savings could be made on less qualified staff.

260. Scott et al. (2001), Table 6. The costs shown in the table (1998 prices) also include extra health care and social benefits, but both of these are relatively small.

261. Rutter et al. (1998).

262. Aos et al. (2001).

Chapter 8: Inequalities

263. The median is the level where 50 per cent are above it and 50 per cent below it. The definition of poverty is that used by Eurostat. Income is measured by income per equivalent adult. In a typical European country 60 per cent of the median income is similar to 50 per cent of the mean (i.e. arithmetic average) income. For a fuller discussion of poverty than this chapter permits, see Bradshaw (2007).

264. Eurostat.

265. Family Resources Survey, 2005/6.

266. Hobcraft (1998), using NCDS. The other factors are family disruption, contact with the police, educational test scores, and fathers' interest in schooling.

267. UNICEF (2007).

268. Wilkinson and Pickett (2009), adapted with their help. The child well-being index excludes the poverty component. Poverty data from the Luxembourg Income Survey (mainly 1999): percentage with less than 60 per cent of median income per equivalent adult. Figures don't match first table.

269. For a careful study of this issue using ALSPAC see Gregg et al. (2008). See also Ford et al. (2004, 2007a), quoted in Chapter 7.

270. Private note for the panel from Jonathan Bradshaw.

271. For a discussion of these issues see Layard (2005).

272. Wilkinson and Pickett (2009).

273. Another way is to correlate the occupational status of parent and child (Erikson and Goldthorpe, 2008). The cross-national rankings are similar when occupational position is measured by a scalar measure of occupational status, to when it is measured by income (as in our graph) (Blanden, 2008).

274. Blanden (2008). The figures are the elasticity of the child's earnings with respect to the father's earnings.

275. Data from Luxembourg Income Study (per cent below 60 per cent of median).

276. Blanden et al. (2004). Non-employed people are excluded. Using an index of social class position, Erikson and Goldthorpe (2008) find no change in social mobility. But the metric of social class at different time periods is less clear than that of income, and any one social class group contains a wide and variable spread of living standards among its numbers (Blanden et al., 2008). There is limited evidence on changes in social mobility in other countries, but, using social class, Breen (2004) shows no improvement in the UK and improvement in all seven other countries in his study.

277. Blanden and Machin (2008).

278. As Erikson and Goldthorpe (2008) point out, social immobility is even higher when it is measured in terms of social class rather than income.

279. Brewer et al. (2008). The series since 1994 are from a different source (FRS) than before 1994 (FES). Overlap data shows that data in 1993 would have been almost two points lower on the current measure.

280. Brewer et al. (2008).

281. Department for Work and Pensions (2008).

282. Sefton and Sutherland (2005), p. 245. This shows that policy changes between 1997 and 2004 reduced the Gini coefficient by about 3 percentage points.

283. Sutherland et al. (2008). Child Benefit and Working Tax Credit are indexed to prices and the family element in tax credits is non-indexed. The child element in tax credits is indexed to earnings.

284. See references in note 18. Note that many of these problems overlap. For example, all the groups identified suffer from disproportionately high levels of child poverty.

285. DCSF (2006).

286. Social Exclusion Unit (2002).

287. DCSF (2006).

288. Chase et al. (2006).

289. They are now meant to receive the Strengths and Difficulties Questionnaire (SDQ) but a proper assessment requires that they receive a more detailed assessment – for example using the Development and Well-Being Assessment (DAWBA), www.dawba.com.

290. In 2006, 58 per cent of men aged 20 to 24 in England lived with their parents compared with 39 per cent of women, an increase of 8 and 7 percentage points respectively from 1991 (ONS, 2007).

291. CRAE (2000).

292. On this paragraph see CRAE (2002).

293. Lader et al. (2000); Chitsabesan et al. (2006).

294. For evidence of what works, see Allen (2006).

295. As an example, if a child in care goes into custody the same social worker should visit him in custody as saw him earlier – not, as now, a different one.

296. For the government's plans see the Youth Crime Action Plan.

297. Platt (2007).

298. Children's Society (2008b).

299. Feinstein and Sabates (2006).

300. MORI (2003).

301. For estimates of the cost, see Hirsch (2006).

Chapter 9: Conclusions

302. World Values Survey. Raw data.

303. DCSF (2007). Note that DWP *Opportunities for All* shows each year what is improving and what is not.

304. World Values Survey. Raw data. In 1999, 64.1 per cent of adults in Denmark, 59.4 per cent in the Netherlands, and 63.7 per cent in Sweden thought that 'most people can be trusted'. The figures were 28.5 per cent for adults in Great Britain and 35.5 per cent for the US.

References

Academy of Medical Sciences (2004) *Calling Time. The Nation's Drinking as a Major Health Issue*, London: Academy of Medical Sciences.

Advisory Council on the Misuse of Drugs (2003) *Hidden Harm: Responding to the Needs of Children of Problem Drug Users*, Report of an inquiry by the Advisory Council on the Misuse of Drugs, London: Home Office.

Advisory Council on the Misuse of Drugs (2007) *Hidden Harm Three Years on: Realities, Challenges and Opportunities*, Report of an inquiry by the Advisory Council on the Misuse of Drugs, London: Home Office.

Ainsworth, M. D., Blehar, M. C., Waters, E. and Wall, S. (1978) *Patterns of Attachment*, Hillsdale, NJ: Erlbaum.

Allen, R. (2006) *From Punishment to Problem-solving: A New Approach to Children in Trouble*, London: Centre for Crime and Justice Studies.

Amato, P. R. (1995) 'Children's adjustment to divorce: Theories, hypotheses and empirical support', *Journal of Marriage and the Family*, 55, 628–40.

Amato, P. R. and Keith, B. (1991) 'Parental divorce and the well-being of children: A meta-analysis', *Psychological Bulletin*, 110, 26–46.

Anderson, C. A., Gentile, D. A. and Buckley, K. E. (2007) *Violent Video Game Effects on Children and Adolescents*, Oxford: Oxford University Press.

Aos, S., Phipps, P., Barnoski, R. and Lieb, R. (2001) *The Comparative Costs and Benefits of Programs to Reduce Crime. Version 4.0*, Olympia: Washington State Institute for Public Policy.

Arseneault, L., Walsh, E., Trzesniewski, K., Newcombe, R., Caspi, A. and Moffitt, T. E. (2006) 'Bullying victimization uniquely contributes to adjustment problems in young children: a nationally representative cohort study', *Pediatrics*, 118, 130–38.

Balding, J. (2007) *Young People into 2007*, Exeter: Schools Health Education Unit.

Baumrind, D. (1971) 'Current patterns of parental authority', *Developmental Psychology Monograph*, 4, 1–103.

REFERENCES

Baumrind, D. (1991) 'The influence of parenting style on adolescent competence and substance use', *Journal of Early Adolescence*, 11, 56–95.

Belsky, J., Vandell, D. L., Burchinal, M., Clarke-Stewart, A., McCartney, K., Owen, M. T. et al. (2007) 'Are there long-term effects of early child care?' *Child Development*, 78, 681–701.

Berndt, T. J., Hawkins, J. A. and Jiao, Z. (1999) 'Influences of friends and friendships on adjustment to junior high school', *Merrill-Palmer Quarterly*, 45, 13–41.

Blackwell, A. and Dawe, F. (2003) *Non-residential Parental Contact Final Report*, Social and Vital Statistics Division, London: Office of National Statistics.

Blanden, J. (2008) 'How much can we learn from international comparisons of social mobility?' Paper for the Sutton Trust – Carnegie Summit on Social Mobility, June, New York.

Blanden, J. and Machin, S. (2008) 'Up and Down the Generational Income Ladder in Britain: Past Changes and Future Prospects', Paper for the Sutton Trust.

Blanden, J., Gregg, P. and Macmillan, L. (2008) 'Intergenerational Persistence in Income and Social Class: The Impact of Within-group-inequality', Mimeo, LSE, Centre for Economic Performance.

Blanden, J., Goodman, A., Gregg, P. and Machin, S. (2004) 'Changes in intergenerational mobility in Britain', in M. Corak (ed.), *Generational Income Inequality*, Cambridge: Cambridge University Press.

Blatchford, P., Goldstein, H., Martin, C. and Browne, W. (2002) 'A study of class size effects in English school reception year classes', *British Educational Research Journal*, 28, 171–87.

Bonell, C., Fletcher, A. and McCambridge, J. (2007) 'Improving school ethos may reduce substance misuse and teenage pregnancy', *British Medical Journal*, 334, 614–16.

Bowlby, J. (1969) *Attachment and Loss. Vol 1: Attachment*, New York: Basic Books.

Bradshaw, J. (2007) 'Investing in children', in C. Willow (ed.), *Advancing Opportunity: Children, Human Rights and Social Justice*, London: The Smith Institute.

Breen, R. (2004) *Social Mobility in Europe*, Oxford: Oxford University Press.

Brewer, M., Muriel, A., Phillips, D. and Sibieta, L. (2008) *Poverty and Inequality in the UK: 2008*, Institute for Fiscal Studies Commentary C105.

Bridges, L. J., Roe, A. E. C., Dunn, J. and O'Connor, T. G. (2007) 'Children's perspectives on their relationships with grandparents following parental separation: A longitudinal study', *Social Development*, 16, 539–54.

REFERENCES

Browne, K. and Hamilton-Giachritis, C. (2005) 'The influence of violent media on children and adolescents: A public-health approach', *Lancet*, 365, 702–10.

Buchanan, A. (2008) *Involved Grandparenting and Child Wellbeing*, ESRC Research Grant Report.

Burgess, A. (2007) 'The Costs and Benefits of Active Fatherhood: Evidence and Insights to Inform the Development of Policy and Practice', Paper prepared by Fathers Direct to inform the DfES/HM Treasury Joint Policy Review on Children and Young People.

Burroughs-Lange, S. (2006) *Evaluation of Reading Recovery in London Schools: Every Child a Reader 2005–6*, Institute of Education, University of London.

Byron, T. (2008) *Safer Children in a Digital World: Report of the Byron Review*, London: Department for Children, Schools and Families and Department for Culture, Media and Sport.

Chase, E., Simon, A. and Jackson, S. (2006) *In Care and After: A Positive Perspective*, London: Routledge.

Chatfield, T. (2008) 'Rage against the machines', *Prospect Magazine*, 147 (June).

Cherlin, A., Furstenberger Jnr, F. F., Chase-Lansdale, P. L., Kiernan, K. E., Robins, P., Morrison, D. R. et al. (1991) 'Longitudinal studies of effects of divorce on children in Great Britain and the United States', *Science*, 252, 1386–9.

Child Rights Alliance for England (CRAE) (2000) *Implementing Children's Rights and Health*.

Child Rights Alliance for England (CRAE) (2002) *Rethinking Child Imprisonment: A Report on Young Offenders Institutions*, London.

Children's Society (2006) *The Good Childhood: Evidence Summary One – Friends*.

Children's Society (2008a) 'Reflections on childhood', www.childrens society.org.uk.

Children's Society (2008b) *Living on the Edge of Despair*, London.

ChildWise (2006) *Monitor: The Trends Report*, Norwich.

Chitsabesan, P., Kroll, L., Bailey, S., Kenning, C., Sneider, S., MacDonald, W. and Theodosiou, L. (2006) 'Mental health needs of young offenders in custody and in the community', *British Journal of Psychiatry*, 188, 534–40.

Clarke-Stewart, A. and Brentano, C. (2006) *Divorce: Causes and Consequences*, New Haven/London: Yale University Press.

Coie, J. D. and Dodge, K. A. (1998) 'Aggression and antisocial behaviour', in W. Damon (ed.), *Handbook of Child Psychology: Social, Emotional and Personality Development*, New York: Wiley.

Collins, W. A. (2003) 'More than myth: The developmental significance of romantic relationships during adolescence', *Journal of Research on Adolescence*, 13, 1–24.

Collishaw, S., Maughan, B., Goodman, R. and Pickles, A. (2004) 'Time trends in adolescent mental health', *Journal of Child Psychology and Psychiatry*, 45, 1350–62.

Collishaw, S., Maughan, B., Goodman, R., Dunn, J. and Pickles, A. (2007) 'Modelling the contribution of changes in family life to time trends in adolescent conduct problems', *Social Science and Medicine*, 65, 2576–87.

Covell, K. and Howe, B. (2005) *Rights, Respect and Responsibility: Report on the RRR Initiative to Hampshire County Education Authority*, Children's Rights Centre, Cape Breton University (Canada).

Currie, C. (ed.), Nic Gabhainn, S., Godeau, E., Roberts, C., Smith, R., Currie, D., Picket, W., Richter, M., Morgan, A. and Barnekow, V. (2008) *Health Behaviour in School Children (HBSC) International Report from the 2005/ 2006 Survey*, Copenhagen: World Health Organization.

Davidson, R. and Harrington, A. (2002) *Visions of Compassion: Western Scientists and Tibetan Buddhists Examine Human Nature*, Oxford: Oxford University Press.

Davies, J. and Brember, I. (1998) 'National Curriculum testing and self-esteem in year 2 – the first five years: A cross-sectional study', *Educational Psychology*, 18, 365–75.

Davies, J. and Brember, I. (1999) 'Reading and mathematics attainments and self-esteem in years 2 and 6: An eight-year cross-sectional study', *Educational Studies*, 25, 145–57.

Day, C., Stobart, G., Sammons, P., Hadfield, M. and Kingston, A. (2004) 'Profiling Variations in Teachers' Work, Lives and Effectiveness: The VITAE Project', Paper presented at the annual British Educational Research Association (BERA) Conference, 16–18 September 2004.

Department for Children, Schools and Families (DCSF) (2006) *Care Matters: Transforming the Lives of Children and Young People in Care*, London.

Department for Children, Schools and Families (DCSF) (2007) *The Children's Plan: Building Brighter Futures*, London.

Department for Education and Skills (DfES) (2004) *Every Child Matters*, London.

Department of Health (2004) *Choosing Health: Making Healthy Choices Easier*, London.

Department of Health (2008) *Improving Access to Psychological Therapies. Implementation Plan: National Guidelines for Regional Delivery*, London.

REFERENCES

Department of Health and Department for Education and Skills (2004) *National Service Framework for Children, Young People and Maternity Services*, London.

Department for Work and Pensions (2008) *No One Written off: Reforming Welfare to Reward Responsibility* (ref Cm 7363), London.

DIUS and DCSF (Department for Innovation, Universities and Skills and Department for Children, Schools and Families) (2008) *World-class Apprenticeships: Unlocking Talent, Building Skills for All*, London.

Dmitrieva, J., Steinberg, L. and Belsky, J. (2007) 'Child-care history, classroom composition, and children's functioning in kindergarten', *Psychological Science*, 18, 1032–9.

Dolton, P. and Newsom, D. (2003) 'The relationship between teacher turnover and school performance', *London Review of Education*, 1, 132–40.

Dunn, J. (1988) *The Beginnings of Social Understanding*, Cambridge, MA: Harvard University Press.

Dunn, J. (2003) 'Contact and children's perspectives on parental relationships', in A. Bainham, B. Lindley, M. Richards and L. Trinder (eds), *Children and Their Families: Contacts, Rights and Welfare* (pp. 15–32), Oxford: Hart Publishing.

Dunn, J. (2004) *Children's Friendships: The Beginnings of Intimacy*, Oxford: Blackwell.

Dunn, J. and Deater-Deckard, K. (2001) *Children's Views of Their Changing Families*, York: Joseph Rowntree Foundation.

Dunn, J., Brown, J. and Beardsall, L. (1991) 'Family talk about feeling states and children's later understanding of others' emotions', *Developmental Psychology*, 27, 448–55.

Dunn, J., Brown, J. R. and Maguire, M. (1995) 'The development of children's moral sensibility: Individual differences and emotion understanding', *Developmental Psychology*, 31, 649–59.

Dunn, J., Cutting, A. and Demetriou, H. (2000) 'Moral sensibility, understanding others, and children's friendship interactions in the preschool period', *British Journal of Developmental Psychology*, 18, 159–77.

Dunn, J., Fergusson, M. and Maughan, B. (2006) 'Grandparents, grandchildren, and family change', in A. Clarke-Stewart and J. Dunn (eds), *Families Count: Effects on Child and Adolescent Development*, Cambridge: Cambridge University Press.

Dunn, J., O'Connor, T. G. and Cheng, H. (2005) 'Children's responses to conflict between their different parents: Mothers, stepfathers, non-resident fathers and non-resident stepmothers', *Journal of Clinical Child and Adolescent Psychology*, 34, 223–34.

Dunn, J., Cheng, H., O'Connor, T. G. and Bridges, L. (2004) 'Children's perspectives on their relationships with their non-resident fathers: Influences, outcomes and implications', *Journal of Child Psychology and Psychiatry*, 45, 553–66.

Dunn, J., Davies, L., O'Connor, T. G. and Sturgess, W. (2001) 'Family lives and friendships: The perspectives of children in step-, single-parent and non-step-families', *Journal of Family Psychology*, 15, 272–87.

Eisenberg, N. and Faber, R. (1998) 'Prosocial development', in W. Damon (ed.), *Handbook of Child Psychology*, New York: Wiley.

Elliott, B. J. and Richards, M. P. M. (1991) 'Children and divorce: Educational performance and behaviour, before and after parental separation', *International Journal of Law and the Family*, 5, 258–76.

Ellwood, D. and Jencks, C. (2004) 'The spread of single-parent families in the United States since 1960', in D. Moynihan, L. Reinwater and T. Smeeding (eds), *Public Policy and the Future of the Family*, New York: Russell Sage Foundation.

Equalities Review (2008) *Fairness and Freedom: The Final Report of the Equalities Review*, London.

Erikson, R. and Goldthorpe, J. (2008) *Income and Class Mobility in between Generations in Great Britain: The Problem of Divergent Findings from the Datasets of Birth Cohort Studies*, Stockholm: Swedish Institute for Social Research.

Farrer, F. (2000) *A Quiet Revolution*, London: Rider.

Feinstein, L., Bynner, J. and Duckworth, K. (2005) *Leisure Contexts in Adolescence and their Effects on Adult Outcomes* (No. 15), London: Centre for Research on the Wider Benefits of Learning.

Feinstein, L. and Sabates, R. (2006) *Predicting Adult Life Outcomes from Earlier Signals: Identifying those at Risk*, Report for the Prime Minister's Strategy Unit, London: Institute of Education.

Fergusson, D., Horwood, J. and Ridder, E. (2005) 'Show me the child at seven: The consequences of conduct problems in childhood for psychosocial functioning in adulthood', *Journal of Child Psychology and Psychiatry*, 46, 837–49.

Ferri, E., Bynner, J. and Wadsworth, M. (2003) *Changing Britain, Changing Lives: Three Generations at the Turn of the Century*, London: Institute of Education Publications.

REFERENCES

Field, T. (1984) 'Separation stress of young children transferring to new schools', *Developmental Psychology*, 20, 786–92.

Fielder, A., Gardner, W., Nairn, A. and Pitt, J. (2007) *Fair Game?* London: National Consumer Council.

Flouri, E. (2005) *Fathering and Child Outcomes*, Chichester: Wiley.

Flouri, E. and Buchanan, A. (2002) 'What predicts good relationships with parents in adolescence and partners in adult life: findings from the 1958 British birth cohort', *Journal of Family Psychology*, 16, 186–98.

Fonagy, P., Target, M., Cottrell, D., Phillips, J. and Kurtz, Z. (2002) *What Works for Whom? A Critical Review of Treatments for Children and Adolescents*, New York and London: Guilford.

Ford, T., Goodman, R. and Meltzer, H. (2004) 'The relative importance of child, family, school and neighbourhood correlates of childhood psychiatric disorder', *Social Psychiatry and Psychiatric Epidemiology*, 39, 487–96.

Ford, T., Collishaw, S., Meltzer, H., and Goodman, R. (2007a) 'A prospective study of childhood psychology: independent predictors of change over three years', *Social Psychiatry and Psychiatric Epidemiology*, 42, 953–61.

Ford, T., Vostanis, P., Meltzer, H. and Goodman, R. (2007b) 'Psychiatric disorder among British children looked after by local authorities: Comparison with children living in private households', *British Journal of Psychiatry*, 190, 319–25.

Frankl, V. (2004) *Man's Search for Meaning*, London: Rider.

Friedman, R. A. (2006) 'Uncovering an epidemic: Screening for mental illness in teens', *New England Journal of Medicine*, 355, 2717–19.

Fuller, F. (2008) *Drug Use, Smoking and Drinking among Young People in England in 2007*, London: National Centre for Social Research and National Foundation for Educational Research.

Furstenberg, F. and Kiernan, K. (2001) 'Delayed parental divorce: How much do children benefit?' *Journal of Marriage and the Family*, 63, 446–57.

Gill, T. (2007) *No Fear: Growing up in a Risk Averse Society*, London: Calouste Gulbenkian Foundation.

Glewwe, P., Ilias, N. and Kremer, M. (2002) 'Teacher Incentives', Mimeo, Washington, DC: Brookings Institution.

Goleman, D. (1995) *Emotional Intelligence*, London: Bloomsbury.

Golombok, S. (2002) 'Adoption by lesbian couples', *British Medical Journal*, 324, 1407–8.

Golombok, S. (2006) 'New family forms', in A. Clarke-Stewart and J. Dunn

REFERENCES

(eds), *Families Count: Effects on Child and Adolescent Development*, Cambridge: Cambridge University Press.

Goodman, R. and Scott, S. (2005) *Child Psychiatry*, Oxford: Blackwell Publishing.

Goodyer, I. M., Wright, C. and Altham, P. M. (1989) 'Recent friendships in anxious and depressed school age children', *Psychological Medicine*, 19, 165–74.

Gottman J. M. (1986) 'The observation of social process', in J. M. Gottman and J. G. Parker (eds), *Conversations of Friends: Speculations on Affective Development*, New York: Cambridge University Press.

Graham, A., Moore, L., Sharp, D. and Diamond, I. (2002) 'Improving teenagers' knowledge of emergency contraception: cluster randomised controlled trial of a teacher led intervention', *British Medical Journal*, 324, 1179.

Graham, P. (2004) *The End of Adolescence*, Oxford: Oxford University Press.

Graves, L., Stratton, G., Ridgers, N. and Cable, N. (2007) 'Energy expenditure in adolescents playing new generation computer games', *British Medical Journal*, 335, 22–9.

Green, H., McGinnity, A., Meltzer, H., Ford, T. and Goodman, R. (2005) *Mental Health of Children and Young People in Great Britain, 2004.* London: Office of National Statistics.

Gregg, P., Propper, C. and Washbrook, E. (2007) *Understanding the Relationship Between Parental Income and Multiple Child Outcomes: A Decomposition Analysis*, Discussion Paper 129, London: Centre for Analysis of Social Exclusion, London School of Economics and Political Science.

Gregg, P., Washbrook, E., Propper, C. and Burgess, S. (2005) 'The effects of a mother's return to work decision on child development in the UK', *Economic Journal*, 115, F48–F80.

Grossman, K., Grossman, K. E., Fremmer-Bombik, E., Kindler, H., Scheurer-Englisch, H. and Zimmermann, P. (2002) 'The uniqueness of the child–father attachment relationship: Fathers' sensitive and challenging play as a pivotal variable in a 16-year-long study', *Social Development*, 11, 307–31.

Grusec, J. (2006) 'The development of moral behaviour and conscience from a socialization perspective', in M. Killen and J. G. Smetana (eds), *Handbook of Moral Development*, Mahwah, NJ: Erlbaum.

Hall, K. and Øzerk, K. (2008) *Primary Curriculum and Assessment: England and Other Countries*, Primary Review Research Survey 3/1, Cambridge: University of Cambridge.

REFERENCES

Hall, P. (1999) 'Social capital in Britain', *British Journal of Politics*, 29, 417–61.

Halpern, D. (2004) *Social Capital*, Cambridge: Polity Press.

Harlen, W. and Deakin Crick, R. (2002) *A Systematic Review of the Impact of Summative Assessment and Tests on Students' Motivation for Learning*, London: EPPI-Centre, Social Science Research Unit, Institute of Education.

Hartup, W. W. and Abecassis, M. (2004) 'Friends and enemies', in P. K. Smith and C. Hart (eds), *Blackwell Handbook of Childhood Social Development*, Oxford: Blackwell Publishers.

Hattie, J. (2003) 'Teachers Make a Difference: What is the Research Evidence?' Paper presented at Australian Council for Educational Research Annual Conference, October 2003.

Henderson, M., Wight, D., Raab, G., Abraham, C., Parkes, A., Scott, S. et al. (2007) 'Impact of a theoretically based sex education programme (SHARE) delivered by teachers on NHS registered conceptions and terminations: final results of cluster randomised trial', *British Medical Journal*, 334, 133.

Hirsch, D. (2006) *What Will it Take to End Child Poverty? Firing on All Cylinders*, York: Joseph Rowntree Foundation.

HM Treasury and DfES (2007a) *Aiming High for Disabled Children: Better Support for Families*, London.

HM Treasury and DfES (2007b) *Policy Review of Children and Young People: A Discussion Paper*, London.

Hobcraft, J. (1998) 'Intergenerational and Life Course Transmission of Social Exclusion', CASE Paper 15, London: London School of Economics.

Hodges, E. V. and Perry, D. G. (1999) 'Personal and interpersonal antecedents and consequences of victimization by peers', *Journal of Personality and Social Psychology*, 76, 677–85.

Hodges, J. and Tizard, B. (1989) 'Social and family relationships of ex-institutional adolescents', *Journal of Child Psychology and Psychiatry*, 30, 77–98.

Hofstede, G. (2000) *Culture's Consequences: Comparing Values, Behaviours, Institutions and Organizations across Nations* (2nd edn), Thousand Oaks: Sage Publications.

Hollis, L. (2002) 'We know what she wants', *Guardian*, 6 November 2002.

Home Office (2008) *Youth Crime Action Plan 2008*, London: Home Office.

Howes, C. (1988) 'Peer interaction of young children', *Monographs of Society for Research in Child Development*, 53.

Howes, C., Hamilton, C. and Phillipsen, L. (1998) 'Stability and continuity of a child–caregiver and child–peer relationships', *Child Development*, 69, 418–26.

Howes, C., Unger, O. and Matheson, C. (1992) *The Collaborative Construction of Pretend: Social Pretend Play Functions*, Albany, NY: State University of New York Press.

Ingham, R. (1998) 'Exploring Interactional Competence: Comparative Data from the United Kingdom and the Netherlands on Young People's Sexual Development', Paper presented at 24th meeting of the International Academy of Sex Research, Sirmione, Italy, 3–6 June.

Jaffee, S. R., Moffitt, T. E., Caspi, A. and Taylor, A. (2003) 'Living with (or without) father: The benefits of living with two biological parents depend on the father's antisocial behaviour', *Child Development*, 74, 109–26.

Joseph Rowntree Foundation (2008) *What are Today's Social Evils?* York.

Kasser, T. (2002) *The High Price of Materialism*, Cambridge MA: MIT Press.

Kiernan, K. (2004) 'Cohabitation and divorce across nations and generations', in P. L. Chase-Lansdale, K. Kiernan, and R. Friedman (eds), *Human Development across Lives and Generations: The Potential for Change*, New York: Cambridge University Press.

Kiernan, K. E. and Huerta, M. C. (2008) 'Economic deprivation, maternal depression, parenting and children's cognitive and emotional development in early childhood', *British Journal of Sociology*, 59.

Kiernan, K. E. and Mensah F. K. (in press) 'Poverty, maternal depression, family status and children's cognitive and behavioural development in early childhood: a longitudinal study', *Journal of Social Policy*.

Kiernan, K. E. and Smith, K. (2003) 'Unmarried parenthood: New insights from the Millennium Cohort Study', *Population Trends*, 114, 23–33.

Killen, M., Margie, N. G. and Sinn, S. (2006) 'Morality in the context of intergroup relationships', in M. Killen and J. G. Smetana (eds), *Handbook of Moral Development*, Mahwah, NJ: Erlbaum.

Kramer, L. and Gottman, J. M. (1992) 'Becoming a sibling: With a little help from my friends', *Developmental Psychology*, 28, 685–99.

Ladd, G. (1999) 'Peer relationships and social competence during early and middle childhood', *Annual Review of Psychology*, 50, 333–59.

Lader, D., Singleton, N. and Meltzer, H. (2000) *Psychiatric Morbidity among Young Offenders in England and Wales*, London: Office for National Statistics.

Lamb, M. E., Sternberg, K. J. and Thompson, R. A. (1999) 'The effects of divorce and custody arrangements on children's behavior, development and adjustment', in M. E. Lamb (ed.), *Parenting and Child Development in 'Non-traditional' Families*, Mahwah, NJ: Erlbaum.

Layard, R. (2005) *Happiness: Lessons for a New Science*, London: Penguin.

Layard, R. (2008) 'Child mental health. Key to a healthier society', see http://cep.lse.ac.uk/Layard.

Lewis, C. and Lamb, M. (2006) *Fatherhood: Connecting the Strands of Diversity across Time and Space*, Report to the Joseph Rowntree Foundation.

Livingstone, S. (2007) 'Evaluating the online risks for children in Europe', *Telos*, 73, 52–69.

Livingstone, S. (2008) 'Children's Media: More Harm than Good?' Public lecture, London School of Economics.

Loehlin, J. C. (1992) *Genes and Environment in Personality Development*, Newbury Park, CA: Sage.

Lord Chancellor's Department (1999) *High Divorce Rates: The State of the Evidence on Reasons and Remedies*, LCD Research Series No. 2/99 (vol. 1), London.

Lovat, T. and Toomey, R. (2007) *Values Education and Quality Teaching*, Sydney: David Barlow Publishing.

Lussier, G., Deater-Deckard, K., Dunn, J. and Davies, L. (2002) 'Support across two generations: Children's closeness to grandparents following parental divorce and remarriage', *Journal of Family Psychology*, 16, 363–76.

Lyubomirsky, S. (2007) *The How of Happiness*, London: Sphere.

Machin, S. and McNally, S. (2008) 'The literacy hour', *Journal of Public Economics*, 92, 1441–62.

Maclean, M. and Eekelaar, J. (1995) *The Parental Obligation: A Study of Parenthood Across Households*, Oxford: Hart Publishing.

Madge, N. and Barker, J. (2007) *Risk and Childhood*, London: RSA Risk Commission.

Make Space Youth Review (2007) *Transforming the Offer for Young People in the UK*, London: 4Children.

Manke, B., McGuire, S., Reiss, D., Hetherington, E. M. and Plomin, R. (1995) 'Genetic contributions to children's extrafamilial social interactions: Teachers, best friends, and peers', *Social Development*, 4, 238–56.

Marsden, J., Boys, A., Farrell, M., Stilwell, G., Hutchings, K., Hillebrand, J. et al. (2005) 'Personal and social correlates of alcohol consumption among mid-adolescents', *British Journal of Developmental Psychology*, 23, 427–50.

Matheson, J. and Summerfield, C. (eds) (2000) *Social Focus on Young People*, London: Office for National Statistics.

Maughan, B., Collishaw, S., Meltzer, H. and Goodman, R. (2008) 'Recent trends in UK child and adolescent mental health', *Social Psychiatry and Psychiatric Epidemiology*, 43, 305–10.

McCormick, B. and Stone, I. (2006) 'The Obesity Explosion: Causes, Costs and Consequences', Department of Health Working Paper, London.

McDonald, A. (2001) 'The prevalence and effects of test anxiety in school children', *Educational Psychology*, 21, 89–101.

McKinsey and Company (2007) *How the World's Best Performing Schools Systems Come out on Top*, London: McKinsey & Co.

McLanahan, S. and Sandefur, G. (1994), *Growing up with a Single Parent*, Cambridge, MA: Harvard University Press.

Meier, S. and Stutzer, A. (2008) 'Is volunteering rewarding in itself?' *Economica*, 75, 39–59.

Mills, C. (2004) *Problems at Home, Problems at School: The Effects of Maltreatment in the Home on Children's Functioning at School. An Overview of Recent Research*, London: NSPCC.

Millwood Hargrave, A. and Livingstone, S. (2006) *Harm and Offence in Media Content: A Review of the Evidence*, Bristol: Intellect Press.

Moffitt, T. (1993) 'Adolescence-limited and life-course-persistent antisocial behaviour: A developmental taxonomy', *Psychological Review*, 100, 674–701.

Monks, C. P., Smith, P. K. and Swettenham, J. (2006) 'Definitions of bullying: Age differences in understanding of the term, and the role of experience', *British Journal of Developmental Psychology*, 24, 801–21.

Moore, T. H., Zammit, S., Lingford-Hughes, A., Barnes, T. R., Jones, P. B., Burke, M. et al. (2007) 'Cannabis use and risk of psychotic or affective mental health outcomes: A systematic review', *Lancet*, 370, 319–28.

MORI (2002) *Quality of Life Indicators Survey*, London.

MORI (2003) *Profiles of Prejudice*, London: MORI and Stonewall.

Mortimore, P. (2007) 'What Is and What Might Be?', Paper given at Education Alliance Conference (March), London: National Union of Teachers.

Mortimore, P., Sammons, P., Stoll, L., Lewis, D. and Ecob, R. (1988) *School Matters: The Junior Years*, Holwell: Open Books.

Moss, P. and Deven, F. (2006) 'Leave policies and research: A cross-national overview', *Marriage and Family Review*, 39, 255–86.

Nairn, A., Ormrod, J. and Bottomley, P. (2007) *Watching, Wanting and Well-being: Exploring the Links. A Study of 9–13-year-olds*, London: National Consumer Council.

REFERENCES

National Family and Parenting Institute (NFPI) (2000) Survey, *Teenagers' Attitudes to Parenting*, London: National Family and Parenting Institute.

National Family and Parenting Institute (NFPI) (2004) *Hard Sell, Soft Targets?* London: National Family and Parenting Institute.

National Institute of Child Health and Human Development – Early Child Care Research Network (NICHD) (2003) 'Does amount of time spent in child care predict socio-emotional adjustment during the transition to kindergarten?' *Child Development*, 74, 976–1005.

Neill, S. (2008) *Disruptive Pupil Behaviour: Its Causes and Effects. An Interim Report*, London: National Union of Teachers.

Newburn, T. (2007) 'Youth crime and youth culture', in M. Maguire, R. Morgan and R. Reiner (eds), *The Oxford Handbook of Criminology* (4th edn), Oxford: Oxford University Press.

Newson, J. and Newson, E. (1970) *Four Years Old in an Urban Community*, Harmondsworth: Penguin Books.

Nickell, S. and Quintini, G. (2002) 'The consequences of the decline in public sector pay in Britain: A little bit of evidence', *Economic Journal*, 112, F107–F118.

Noden, P. and West, A. (2008) 'Expenditure on Education over the Life Course', Mimeo, LSE Education Research Group.

Noret, N. and Rivers, I. (2006), 'The Prevalance of Bullying by Text Message or Email: Results of a Four Year Study', Presented at the British Psychological Society Annual Conference, Cardiff City Hall.

Normoyle, H. (2008) *Children, Young People and Online Content*, London: Ofcom.

O'Brien, M. (2005) *Shared Caring: Bringing Fathers into the Frame*, Manchester: Equal Opportunities Commission.

OECD (1995) *Literacy, Economy and Society*, Paris: Organization for Economic Cooperation and Development.

OECD (2007) *PISA 2006: Science Competencies for Tomorrow's World*, Paris: Organization for Economic Cooperation and Development.

OECD (2008) *Jobs for Youth: United Kingdom*, Paris: Organization for Economic Cooperation and Development.

Ofcom (2006) *Media Literacy Audit: Report on Media Literacy Among Children*, London.

Ofcom (2007) *The Future of Television Programming: Research Report*, London.

Office for National Statistics (ONS) (2000) *National Diet and Nutrition Survey: Young People Aged 4–18 years. Vol. 1: Report of the Diet and Nutrition Survey*, London.

REFERENCES

Office for National Statistics (ONS) (2005) *General Household Survey, 2005*, London.

Office for National Statistics (ONS) (2007) *Social Trends*, 37, London.

Office for National Statistics (ONS) (2008) *Social Trends*, 38, London.

Olweus, D. (1993) *Bullying at School: What we Know and What we Can Do*, Oxford: Blackwell Publishers.

Palmer, S. (2006) *Toxic Childhood*, London: Orion.

Pardoen, J. and Pijpers, R. (2006) *Verliefd op Internet (In love on the Web)*, Amsterdam: SWP Publishers.

Park, A., Phillips, M. and Johnson, M. (2004) *Young People in Britain: The Attitudes and Experiences of 12 to 19 Year Olds*, London: Department for Education and Science.

Pelkonen, M., Marttunen, M. and Aro, H. (2003) 'Risk for depression: A 6-year follow-up of Finnish adolescents', *Journal of Affective Disorders*, 77, 41–51.

Pike, A. and Atzaba-Poria, N. (2003) 'Do sibling and friend relationships share the same temperamental origins? A twin study', *Journal of Child Psychology and Psychiatry*, 44, 598–611.

Pitts, J. (2008) *Reluctant Gangsters: The Changing Face of Youth Crime*, Uffculme: Willan Publishing.

Platt, L. (2007) *Poverty and Ethnicity in the UK*, Bristol: Policy Press and the Joseph Rowntree Foundation.

Pleck, J. and Masciadrelli, B. P. (2004) 'Paternal involvement by US resident fathers: levels, sources and consequences', in M. E. Lamb (ed.), *The Role of the Father in Child Development*, Chichester: Wiley.

Plomin, R. (1990) 'The role of inheritance in behaviour', *Science*, 248, 183–8.

Povey, D., Coleman, K., Kaiza, P., Hoare, J. and Jansson, K. (2008) *Home Office Statistical Bulletin: Homicides, Firearm Offences and Intimate Violence 2006/07*, (3rd edn), London: Home Office.

Prais, S. J. (1995) *Productivity, Education and Training: An International Perspective*, Cambridge: Cambridge University Press.

Pryor, J. and Rogers, B. (2001) *Children in Changing Families: Life after Parental Separation*, Oxford: Blackwell Publishers.

Putnam, R. (2000) *Bowling Alone: The Collapse and Revival of American Community*, New York: Simon & Schuster.

Reilly, J., Methven, E., McDowell, Z. C., Hacking, B., Alexander, D., Stewart, L. et al. (2003) 'Health consequences of obesity', *Archives of Disease in Childhood*, 88, 748–52.

Reivich, K., Gillham, J., Shatte, A. and Seligman, M. (2005) *A Resilience Initiative and Depression Prevention Program for Youth and Their Parents*, Positive Psychology Center, University of Pennsylvania.

Ridge, T. (2002) *Childhood Poverty and Social Exclusion from a Child's Perspective*, Bristol: Policy Press.

Ridley, M. (1996) *The Origins of Virtue*, London: Penguin.

Rigby, K. (2002) 'Bullying in children', in P. K. Smith and C. Hart (eds), *Blackwell Handbook of Childhood Social Development* (pp. 549–68), Oxford: Blackwell.

Robson, K. and Feinstein, L. (2007) *Leisure Contexts in Adolescence and Their Effects on Adult Outcomes: A More Complete Picture* (Discussion Paper 07–06), London: Centre for Research on the Wider Benefits of Learning. Research Report 15.

Royal College of Psychiatrists/Royal College of Physicians (2000) *Drugs: Dilemmas and Choices*, London: Gaskell.

Royal Society of Arts (2007) *Commission on Illegal Drugs, Communities and Public Policy*, London: Royal Society of Arts.

Runciman, R. (2000) *Report of the Independent Inquiry into the Misuse of Drugs Act 1971*, London: Police Foundation.

Rundle, K., Layte, R. and McGee, H. (2008) *The Irish Study of Sexual Health and Relationships, Sub-report 1: Learning About Sex and First Sexual Experiences*, Dublin: Crisis Pregnancy Agency and the Department of Health and Children.

Rutter, M., Giller, H. and Hagell, A. (1998) *Antisocial Behaviour by Young People*, Cambridge: Cambridge University Press.

Rutter, M., Kreppner, J. and Sonuga-Barke, E. (2008a) 'Attachment insecurity, disinhibited attachment, and attachment disorders: Where do research findings leave the concepts?' *Journal of Child Psychology and Psychiatry.*

Rutter, M., Bishop, D., Pine, D., Scott, S., Stevenson, J., Taylor, E. et al. (2008b) *Child and Adolescent Psychiatry* (5th edn), Oxford: Blackwell Publishing.

Rutter, M., Maughan, B., Mortimore, P., Ouston, J. and Smith, A. (1979) *Fifteen Thousand Hours: Secondary Schools and their Effects on Children*, London: Open Books.

Sammons, P., Elliott, K., Sylva, K., Melhuish, E. C., Siraj-Blatchford, I. and Taggart, B. (2004) 'The impact of pre-school on young children's cognitive attainment at entry to reception', *British Education Research Journal*, 30, 691–712.

Sammons, P., Taggart, B., Siraj-Blatchford, I., Sylva, K., Melhuish, E. and

REFERENCES

Barran, S. (2006) *Variations in Teacher and Pupil Behaviour in Year 5 Classes* (Rep. No. RB817), London: DfES/Institute of Education, University of London.

Sammons, P., Sylva, K., Melhuish, E., Siraj-Blatchford, I., Taggart, B., Barreau, S. et al. (2007) *Influences on Children's Development and Progress in Key Stage 2: Social/Behavioural Outcomes in Year 5*, London: DfES/Institute of Education, University of London.

Sammons, P., Sylva, K., Melhuish, E., Siraj-Blatchford, I. et al. (2008a) *The Influence of School and Teaching Quality on Children's Progress in Primary School* (Rep. No. RB028), London: DCSF.

Sammons, P., Sylva, K., Siraj-Blatchford, I., Taggart, B., Smees, R. and Melhuish, E. (2008b) *Effective Pre-school and Primary Education 3–11 Project (EPPE 3–11): Influences on Pupils' Self-perceptions in Primary School: Enjoyment of School, Anxiety, Isolation and Self-image in Year 5*, London: Institute of Education, University of London.

Sanders, M., Markie-Dadds., C. and Turner, K. (2003) 'Theoretical, scientific and clinical foundations of the Triple P-Positive Parenting Program: A population approach to the promotion of parenting competence', *Parenting Research and Practice Monograph No 1*, University of Queensland, Parenting and Family Support Centre.

Sanders, W. L. and Rivers, J. C. (1996) *Cumulative and Residual Effects of Teachers on Future Student Academic Achievement*, Value-Added Research and Assessment Center, University of Tennessee.

Schaffer, H. R. (2004) *Introducing Child Psychology*, Oxford: Blackwell Publishing.

Scheerens, J. and Bosker, R. (1997) *The Foundations of Educational Effectiveness*, Oxford: Pergamon.

Schnieder, B. H., Atkinson, L. and Tardif, C. (2001) 'Child–parent attachment and children's peer relations: A quantitative review', *Developmental Psychology*, 37, 86–100.

Schor, J. (1998) *The Overspent American*, New York: Basic Books.

Schor, J. (2004) *Born to Buy*, New York: Scribner.

Scott, J. (2004) 'Family, gender and educational attainment in Britain: A longitudinal study', *Journal of Comparative Family Studies* (September), 565–89.

Scott, S. (2005) 'Do parenting programmes for severe child anti-social behaviour work over the longer term, and for whom? 1 year follow up of a multi-centre controlled trial', *Behavioural and Cognitive Psychotherapy*, 33, 403–21.

REFERENCES

Scott, S., Knapp, M., Henderson, J. and Maughan, B. (2001) 'Financial cost of social exclusion: follow-up study of antisocial children into adulthood', *British Medical Journal*, 323, 1–5.

Seawell, M. (1998) *National Television Violence Study* (vol. 3), Thousand Oaks, CA: Sage Publications.

Sefton, T. and Sutherland, H. (2005) 'Inequality and poverty under New Labour', in J. Hills and K. Stewart (eds), *A More Equal Society?* Bristol: Policy Press.

Shanahan, L., Copeland, W., Costello, E. and Angold, A. (2007) 'Specificity of putative psychological risk factors for psychiatric disorders in children and adolescents', *Journal of Child Psychology and Psychiatry*, 49(1), 34–42.

SHEU (2004) *Young People and Physical Activity, Attitudes to Participation and Exercise in Sport 1987–2003*, Exeter: Schools Health Education Unit.

Sigle-Rushton, W., Hobcraft, J. and Kiernan, K. (2005) 'Parental disruption and adult well-being: A cross cohort comparison', *Demography*, 43(3), 427–46.

Singleton, N., Bumpstead, R., O'Brien, M., Lee, A. and Meltzer, H. (2001) *Psychiatric Morbidity Among Adults Living in Private Households, 2000*, London: HMSO.

Sloper, P., Rabiee, P. and Beresford, B. (2007) 'Outcomes for disabled children', *Research Works*, 2, Social Policy Research Unit, University of York.

Smith, P. K. and Shu, S. (2000) 'What good schools can do about bullying', *Childhood*, 7, 193–212.

Smith, P. K., Ananiadou, K. and Cowie, H. (2003) 'Interventions to reduce school bullying', *Canadian Journal of Psychiatry*, 48, 521–99.

Smith, P. K., Pepler, D. and Rigby, K. (2004) *Bullying in Schools: How Successful Can Interventions Be?* Cambridge: Cambridge University Press.

Smith, P. K., Mahdavi, J., Carvalho, M., Fisher, S., Russell, S. and Tippett, N. (2008) 'Cyberbullying: Its nature and impact in secondary school pupils', *Journal of Child Psychology and Psychiatry*, 49, 376–85.

Social Exclusion Unit (1999) *Teenage Pregnancy*, London.

Social Exclusion Unit (2002) *Reducing Re-offending by Ex-prisoners*, London.

Steedman, H., McIntosh, S. and Green, A. (2004) *International Comparisons of Qualifications: Skills Audit Uptake* (Research Report No. RR548), London: DfES.

Strategy Unit (2004) *Alcohol Harm Reduction Strategy for England*, London: Cabinet Office.

224

REFERENCES

Sutherland, H., Evans, M., Hancock, R., Hills, J. and Zantamio, F. (2008) *The Impact of Benefits and Tax Uprating on Income and Poverty*, York: Joseph Rowntree Foundation.

Sylva, K., Melhuish, E., Sammons, P., Siraj-Blatchford, I. and Taggart, B. (2004) *The Effective Provision of Pre-School Education (EPPE) Project: Final Report*, London: DfES/Institute of Education, University of London.

Turk, J., Graham, P. and Verhulst, F. (2007) *Child and Adolescent Psychiatry: A Developmental Approach*, Oxford: Oxford University Press.

Turning Point (2006) *Bottling It up: The Effects of Alcohol Misuse on Children, Parents and Families*, London: Turning Point.

Udry, J. R. (2003) *The National Longitudinal Study of Adolescent Health (Add Health)*, Chapel Hill, NC: Carolina Population Center, University of North Carolina.

UNICEF (2007) *Child Poverty in Perspective. An Overview of Child Well-being in Rich Countries*, Florence: UNICEF Innocenti Research Centre.

Viding, E., Larsson, H. and Jones, A. P. (2008) 'Quantitative genetic studies of antisocial behaviour', *Philosophical Transactions of the Royal Society B*, 363, 2519–27.

Waldfogel, J. (2006) *What Children Need*, Cambridge, MA: Harvard University Press.

Weare, K. (2000) *Promoting Mental, Emotional and Social Learning: A Whole School Approach*, London: Routledge.

Weare, K. and Gray, G. (2003) *What Works in Developing Children's Emotional and Social Competence and Wellbeing?* (Rep. No. RR456), London: DfES.

Webley, P., Burgoigne, C., Lea, S. E. G. and Young, B. (2001) *The Economic Psychology of Everyday Life*, Philadelphia, PA: Psychology Press.

Webster-Stratton, C., Hollinsworth, T. and Kolpacoff, M. (1989) 'The long-term effectiveness and clinical significance of three cost-effective training programs for families with conduct-problem children', *Journal of Consulting and Clinical Psychology*, 57, 550–53.

Weissberg, R. (2007) 'Social and Emotional Learning for Student Success', Paper presented at the CASEL (Collaborative for Academic, Social and Emotional Learning) Forum: Education, All Children for Social, Emotional, and Academic Excellence: From Knowledge to Action, 10 December 2007.

Wellings, K., Field, J., Johnson, A. and Wadsworth, J. (1994) *Sexual Behaviour in Britain*, London: Penguin Books.

Wellings, K., Nanchahal, K., Macdowall, W., McManus, S., Erens, B. et al.

(2001) 'Sexual behaviour in Britain. Early heterosexual experiences', *Lancet*, 358, 1843–50.

Wells, J. E., Horwood, L. J. and Fergusson, D. M. (2006) 'Stability and instability in alcohol diagnosis from ages 18 to 21 and ages 21 to 25 years', *Drug and Alcohol Dependence*, 81, 157–65.

West, P. and Sweeting, H. (2003) 'Fifteen, female and stressed: Changing patterns of psychological distress over time', *Journal of Child Psychology and Psychiatry*, 44, 399–411.

WHO (2008) *Inequalities in Young People's Health: International Report from the HBSC 2006/07 Survey, Health Policy for Children and Adolescents*, Copenhagen: World Health Organization Regional Office for Europe.

Wight, D., Henderson, M., Raab, G., Abraham, C., Buston, K., Scott, S. et al. (2000) 'Extent of regretted sexual intercourse among young teenagers in Scotland: A cross sectional survey', *British Medical Journal*, 320, 1243–4.

Wilkinson, R. and Pickett, K. (2009) *The Spirit Level: Why More Equal Societies Almost Always Do Better*, London: Penguin.

Williams, P. (2008) *Independent Review of Mathematics Teaching in Early Years Settings and Primary Schools*, London: DCSF.

Wilson S., Benton, T., Scott, E. and Kendall, L. (2007) *London Challenge: Survey of Pupils and Teachers 2006*, Slough: National Foundation for Educational Research.

Wolpert, M., Fuggle, P., Cottrell, D., Fonagy, P., Phillips, J., Pilling, S., Stein, S. and Target, M. (2006) *Drawing on the Evidence: Advice for Mental Health Professionals Working with Children and Adolescents*, CAMHS.

Woodall, K. and Woodall, N. (2007) *Putting Children First: A Handbook for Separated Parents*, London: Piatkis.

Woodward, L. J. and Fergusson, D. M. (1999) 'Childhood peer relationship problems and psychosocial adjustment in late adolescence', *Journal of Abnormal Child Psychology*, 27, 87–104.

Wright, R. (1994) *The Moral Animal*, New York: Pantheon.

Zahn-Wexler, C., Robinson, J. L. and Emde, R. N. (1992) 'The development of empathy in twins', *Developmental Psychology*, 28, 1038–47.

Index

Page numbers in *italic* refer to figures and tables.

she's not my child, so who cares?

We do. When children feel excluded, isolated or abandoned, The Children's Society provides immediate and lasting support. We alone can't help every child enjoy a good childhood; that is the responsibility of all of us.

Help us create change!

**visit www.makechildhoodbetter.org.uk
or call 0845 300 1128**

We care. You care. Together we can make childhood better for all children.